Wings ot Her

Alaska Bush & Glacier Pilot, Kitty Banner

Dreams

Ann Lewis Cooper with
Bob & Kitty Banner Seemann

To the wings of your dreams!

Kitty Banner Seemann

Commander James A. Lovell Jr.
NASA Astronaut, Apollo 13
   "The world has historically looked upon aviation as a man's domain. Names like Wright, Doolittle, and Lindbergh seem to dominate the field of aviation. But this book tells a different story. Here you will find the adventures of Kitty Banner, who battles the weather and terrain as an Alaskan Bush and Glacier pilot."

Warren Miller
Extreme Sport, Ski Filmmaker, Iconic Ski Storyteller
   Freedom Foundation, wrote; "The first time I met Kitty was at a party in Vail, Colorado. I don't know the exact date; however, I do know that a lot of people talk at me and when Kitty started telling me some of the things she did as a bush pilot, the evening ended way to soon. Every time I saw her in Vail I would bug her about telling of her bush piloting days... In my travels I have heard a lot of great stories and hers always remained at the top of my list to someday see in print. I'm glad it finally happened."

Sir Edmund Hillary
New Zealand mountaineer, explorer, and philanthropist
First confirmed climber to reach the summit of Mount Everest
   In his documentary featuring John Denver and Kitty Banner, Renowned mountaineer Sir Edmund Hillary said, "This is a film about flying dangerous missions in Alaska, an unspoiled wilderness, the home of adventure. Alaska Bush Pilots are skillful pilots who fly tiny planes in the most perilous of conditions. They live by their wits: Taking risks: Landing in seemingly impossible spots, Air dropping, and Performing daring rescues. Both men and women, the Bush Pilots are the vital transportation and communication links.
   "Hunters and fisherman regularly call on the service of a bush pilot to transport then into remote sites. ...Kitty Banner has been a bush pilot running a charter company in one of Alaska's most inaccessible areas. She has a reputation as an exceptional pilot; But, don't let the picture post- card beauty surprise you. Much of remote, rugged Alaska is accessible only by air."

Roberta Sheldon
Aviation Pioneer, Native Alaskan, Talkeetna Community Council Chair,
Environmentalist, and Author
   "When I met Kitty in Talkeetna so many years ago, I saw a young lady who was vibrant, dynamic, beautiful (inside as well as outside), and who extended a genuine friendliness to all she met. She struck me as one of a kind. It was fairly early in her flying career at the time, but she sure knew her stuff and was eagerly looked forward to each new phase that she was determined to master. A great friendship evolved between us."

WINGS OF HER

Alaska Bush & Glacier Pilot, Kitty Banner

Dreams

Ann Lewis Cooper with
Bob & Kitty Banner Seemann

An Imprint of Finney Company
www.finneyco.com

Dedication

This book is dedicated to my True North and husband, Bob Seemann
and to my adventurous and spirited aviator sons, Mick and Corey.

Contents

Once you have tasted flight,
you will forever walk the earth
with your eyes turned skyward,
for there you have been, and there
you will always long to return.

-Leonardo da Vinci

Jan Carter photo

Acknowledgments

A deep thank you to my husband and best friend, Bob Seemann, for his encouragement, patience, and persistence. Without his constant writing and editing, this book would have never made it to print.

To our best friends, our incredible two sons, Mick and Corey, who encourage us every day to be young at heart and to live life to its fullest.

Special thanks to my extended family friend, Kate Sheldon for her enthusiasm to share her vibrant home town of Talkeetna and the many adventures that we've had together. For her detailed accounts from interviews with many Talkeetna aviators and residents. Also, for her encouragement to help me begin the startup of this book with her descriptive writing.

A special thanks to my dear friend Pat Peeples, President and Founder of Peeples Ink, who loves to fly through edits. Her encouragement, vision, expertise and her true belief in this story helped bring this book to fruition.

Thank you to Amy Laboda, Jacqueline Bowler, Shirley Welch, and Sarah FitzSimmons for their skilled editorial contributions. A very special thanks to Alyssa Clark for her superb final edit. To Sonya Boushek for her exceptional photographic and text layout work and to Brent Bingham for digitizing all of my slides and pictures presented on these pages.

To Al Krysan, Finney Company Inc., I am so grateful for his unending patience throughout the long process to bring this book to his desk.

My thanks to Charlie Cooper, writer and adventurer who traveled to Talkeetna with Ann to research stories of my years flying in Alaska. Sharon Rajnus, thank you for your beautiful glacier and aviation watercolor art. John Luchin, Founder and Principal of Classic Interactions and previous Chief of the Exhibits Division at the National Museum of the United States Air Force, thank you for your early work on this book.

A heartfelt thank you to Kimball Forrest, Doug Geeting, Don Lee, Jim Okonek and Tony Martin, my kindred spirits in Alaskan aviation, for allowing me to share our many special adventures together in this book. Your combined sense of humors helped shed levity and perspective on our ever-changing flying endeavors, along with raucous laughter recounting stories back at the Fairview Bar.

To my brothers, Denny Banner, who first mentored me in the world of aviation with his skill and professionalism and pure joy of flying, thank you for your guidance that helped me reach my personal goals. And thanks to John Banner for his shared enthusiasm that flying is a form of freedom. His shared love of adventure flying inspired my aviation journey.

A big thank you to the wonderful friends that encouraged me from the beginning to complete my story: to the late Roberta Sheldon, the great story teller, who I know is present; Warren Miller, Kathy Sullivan, Holly Sheldon, Kathleen Buchan, Peggy Larson Fuller, Scott Thorburn and Cyndi Nelson, Lida Lafferty, Lili Metcalf, Holly Byers and to all who shared in my flying experiences.

Jim Balog Photo, 1986

Foreword

The Sheldon family - Roberta, Kate, Holly and Robert - were among the first of my friends in Talkeetna, Alaska in 1976. Without Kate's and Ann Cooper's comprehensive and diligent efforts to interview fellow pilots and local Talkeetnans to compile the stories and accounts of my years flying in Alaska, this memoir would never have been written.

Many thanks to the special breed of bush pilots, friends and community of "beautiful downtown Talkeetna". I have worked on this memoir with help from a village of experts. I present it with sincere thanks to all for their contributions.

With all my heart, I thank Ann Cooper. Her aviation knowledge and extraordinary writing expertise was instrumental in bringing this life adventure alive on paper.

These recollections go well beyond cataloging my experiences in Alaska; they highlight adventures, demonstrate character, and denote relationships born of mutual admiration, affection and trust. I wish I would have personally known Don Sheldon, a "living legend" among bush pilots who pioneered many of the glacier landings and who, with his wife Roberta, owned Talkeetna Air Service.

It was through the supportive friendship of the Sheldon's, and many others, that I succeeded beyond my wildest imagination.

Here's to the winds of the world and the wings of your dreams...

Sharon Rajnus, artist

Preface

Kitty and Ann Cooper

By Ann Lewis Cooper

In 1966, Chicago teenager Kitty Banner received a thin hardcover book from Mariann Kelly. The hardbound, gold-covered volume with its mere fifty-six pages was small enough to fit snugly in her hand, while its pithy motivational messages were great enough to inspire the major accomplishments of her life.

The Art of Living, written by Wilferd A. Peterson, was a series of essays that provided a veritable treasure trove of inspirational philosophy and gave form and content to Kitty's life. The book became her constant companion. She read it, referred to it, starred and underlined pertinent passages, jotted notes in its margins, added personal thoughts and elevated it to an essential role in her formative years and beyond. *The Art of Living* became a guide to her adventurous life.

Peterson's advice became Kitty Banner's mantra, her joyous quest in living life to its fullest each day. These uplifting fundamentals of the good life led to Kitty's practiced conduct. They provoked deep thoughts about the meaning of life and her place in it. Through these inspiring words of wisdom, she adapted her philosophy, her faith and her wisdom.

Mount McKinley, ALASKA

To the Summit

By Tony Martin

During takeoff, the Cessna 185's propeller creates a deafening roar. At 2,850 rpm, red line on the tachometer, the prop tip is traveling at close to the speed of sound. A quick glance at the engine instruments indicates that all systems are functioning properly, and as the aircraft accelerates, the empennage (tail section) rises, and with a slight nudge to the controls, the plane is airborne.

On a direct flight, the landing strip on the southeast fork of the Kahiltna Glacier is 35 minutes away from the village of Talkeetna. Most of that time is spent climbing to 8,500 feet, a minimum safe crossing altitude over One Shot Pass. Even on a clear day, that does not seem enough. And with an overcast sky, the notch between ridge top and cloud bottom will appear dark and ominous.

If that gap is completely obscured, sometimes there is a way around Avalanche Spire by means of Second Shot Pass. And if a mixture of ice, rock and fog blocks that way, the possibility is to go by the Long Way - around the low-lying Peters and Dutch Hills to the south and then up over the 36 mile-long Kahiltna Glacier.

There are some days when the questions nag persistently. Which route will be open? How much room will there be in which to maneuver? Are there whiteout conditions up the glacier? What are the winds and visibility at base camp? Can a landing be made safely? How fast is the weather changing? Can the plane be unloaded and reloaded before the passes close or will it be necessary to spend the night in a tent like a would-be mountain climber?

On some days, the mountains are cold, inhospitable and treacherous. But on other days, when the air is impossibly still and the alpenglow sparkles with fire on the granite and ice peaks, an 'Alice-in-Wonderland' effect takes place. Then, in a miniature flying machine, it is possible to wander in peace through the interstices of the majestic crystals that make up the Alaska Range.

The plane climbs slowly because of the weight. It has become an art to pack three climbers and their expeditionary gear, enough for a month in arctic conditions, into the small cabin area of the single engine aircraft. We pass over the Parks Highway, a solid line of demarcation between the advance of the American civilization and the wilderness beyond. Westward 400 miles to the edge of the North American continent there are no interconnecting roads. But while the land below abounds with an endless array of curious facts, the climbers' attentions are focused on the mountains ahead, especially the summit peak of McKinley.

That large mountain toward which we're headed is called Foraker. The twin-peaked mountain between McKinley and Foraker is Mt. Hunter. Those large granite rocks are Moose's Tooth and Broken Tooth. They are over 40 air miles away, but the mountains are deceptive. They seem close enough to touch. The airplane is cramped and the occupants must look over each other's shoulders to get a view. The shutter of a camera clicks monotonously.

The jagged mountains below and to the right are the Tokoshas. That light brown area next to them is the terminus of the Ruth Glacier. The valley up ahead is called the Kanikula and the one intersecting it is the Tokositna. That group of hills to the left is known as "Little Switzerland."

On a nice day and at the right angle, it is possible to point out in the distance the Great Gorge of the Ruth Glacier. The panorama is more spectacular than the Grand Canyon and on that nice day, the scene can be so intense that it is better to be silent and to point only with the wing tip. To those unfamiliar with the route, a passageway through the mountains is not seen until nearly through One Shot Pass. If snowstorms march up the Kahiltna Glacier, there is one less worry. At a jagged and crevassed icefall, the descent must be initiated. It takes about 50 strokes to pump down the hydraulically activated skis. As each lock into place, there is a noticeable thud. Those are the skis coming down.

With that statement, the climbers grow aware they are about to leave the wonderful, eerie world of air to begin their battles with the mountain, the elements and eventually, themselves.

Two grey outcroppings of rock at the base of Mt. Foraker mark the turn to final. All around is a sea of white. Base camp is around the corner. If you look closely, you'll see the trail to Kahiltna Pass. That's the saddle straight ahead. Those dots are climbers. You can't see Windy Corner from here, but the fixed lines are on that shoulder. There's Denali Pass.

Each year, over 700 people try to reach the top of Mt. McKinley. Some will make the summit. Some will injure themselves in the attempt and some will die. Most opt to be flown to the 7100-foot elevation on the southeast fork of the Kahiltna to try the "easy way" to 20,310 feet via the West Buttress route.

Base camp is sprinkled with a multitude of colored tents. Black plastic bags mark the landing strip. On a day with good lighting, a landing can be deceptively easy. But when it's a "little white out," touchdown becomes a sporting proposition. The bags will float in white space as depth perception deteriorates. In the flat light, the decision to land or not is always a matter of judgment, and sometimes the answer is: 'Well, it's not as bad as the last time.'

There are no firm rules on the glacier. Because of the slope's angle, the landing area seems shorter than it actually is. At a certain elevation, there is no room to go around, the approach is one way. Touchdown can be as smooth as silk or a wild ride through the ruts, depending upon the snow conditions. On a hot day when the snow turns to slush, it is impossible to taxi the airplane uphill to turn it around until it has been unloaded.

During climbing season, April through July, base camp is an international conglomeration of aspirin and worn out climbers. Despite the pandemonium, the base camp manager and expedition coordinator on Mt. McKinley, Frances Randall, who tends the radio and registers the visitors, is amazingly calm. Frances, known worldwide in climbing circles, directs the traffic with the same aplomb with which she plays a concert violin. Everyone stops to watch the plume of an avalanche and the comings and goings of an airplane. It takes five minutes to unload the aircraft. The desire to socialize, drink tea and bask in the sun can be tempting. Luckily, there are no cases of frostbite, no rescues to discuss and no parties in difficulty. But those who wish to leave are as eager as those who have just arrived and more climbers wait impatiently in Talkeetna. The exchange is routine.

Takeoff is a rollercoaster ride, and only at the last bump does the airplane want to fly. An aborted takeoff means a long walk uphill for the passengers and new ski tracks through deep snow over unknown crevasses for the pilot. On occasion, after becoming airborne, the climbers will clap.

Whether they made it to the summit or not, they are glad to be free of the mountain's stern grip. On the way back, there is always the opportunity for conversation. Climbers are not dull people.

"Did you make it to the top?" Most heads will shake, No. But a grin in any language means, Yes.

Downhill, the airplane cruises at 150 mph and Talkeetna, only 25 minutes beyond One Shot Pass, is in a different world, where the colors and odors of spring are commonplace and where time begins to be measured, not by the rise and fall of mountains, but on the face of a clock. The flight is sometimes too short. But, it is always interesting. And it is never the same.

From Kitty's Diary:

Thinking

To paraphrase Peterson: "A thinker recognizes the sovereign control of her own mind and... thinks for herself, considers the evidence, seeks the truth, and builds her life upon it... The thinker creates ideas with humility, knowing that behind the idea that she calls her own are the thoughts and efforts of many. She strives to develop a mature mind without losing the simplicity of childhood."

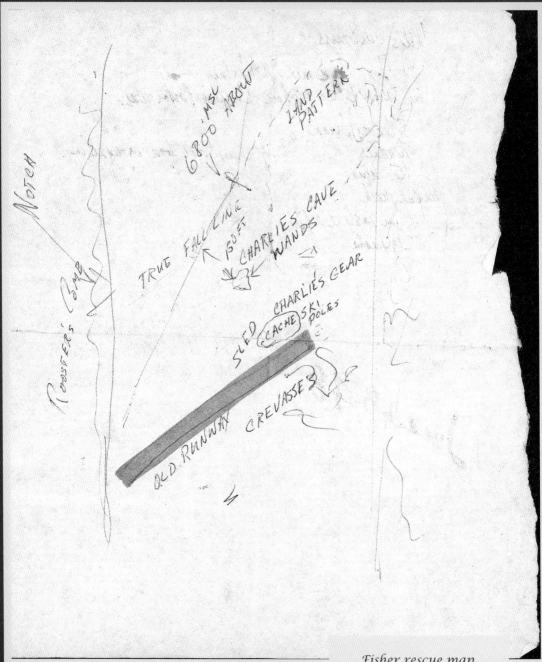

Fisher rescue map,
West Fork, Ruth Glacier

AVALANCHE!

From Kitty's Diary:

The devastating threat inherent in snow-covered, sharply rugged mountains proved to be another stark reality around Denali. It is the lofty snow-covered mountain that boasts the highest peak on the North American continent, now officially returned to its Athabascan title, Denali.

On June 28, 1978, Jim Sharp, owner of Talkeetna Air Taxi (TAT), and I shuttled two airplanes between 6:30 a.m. and 12:30 p.m. for the purpose of moving 23 people and their gear up to the southeast fork of the Kahiltna Glacier. I had flown five Super Cub flights into the southeast fork that morning. After a busy day of flying, I expected the workday to be over. Yet that afternoon, I was tasked with one more flight, one that would prove to be a challenge I'd not soon forget.

One week earlier, Mike Fisher, my Alaskan flight instructor, had flown into the west fork of the Ruth Glacier to pick up Charlie Porter, the famed mountaineer known for his inventive mountaineering equipment. As Fisher landed and attempted to turn the aircraft for the subsequent takeoff, the Cessna 185 became stuck in the deep snow on the 6800-foot glacier landing area. Several attempts at digging out the plane only seemed to bury it in deeper. Weather rapidly moved in and it began to snow heavily. Without radio reception, they knew that they must wait until their plane became overdue and someone would come looking for them.

Charlie and Mike scooped out a snow shelter and pitched their tent for the evening to protect themselves from the cold. But by the end of the second day, the harsh weather conditions remained strong and no plane had come. Neither did a plane come the day after that. Six days passed and the snow did not cease to pummel the mountain. The two men remained on the glacier with very limited supplies. They shared the last of the freeze-dried food that Charlie had with him and used the remaining fuel to melt snow for their water. Yet what really got them through the days was their witty storytelling.

Humor is absolutely necessary in dealing with the almost surreal conditions of glacier piloting. Later at the Ol' Fairview Bar, where they would come to recount their stories and share a laugh, they would reveal that in the freezing temperatures they had to share one sleeping bag and survive off a handful of lemon drops.

The day before, on the 27th, the whiteout weather finally lifted. Jim Sharp flew over the two stranded men that morning. He made contact with them on the CB radio and confirmed that they were okay. They agreed that he would return after he had moved an injured climber and the overdue expeditions from the Kahiltna Base Camp. Later that afternoon, Sharp returned in the Cub to the West Fork. The three men dug out the buried plane. Sharp then flew the C185 out with Porter. Fisher followed in the Cub back to Talkeetna, leaving behind the climbing equipment, now heavier with its accrual of ice and snow.

The next day, returning from my fifth glacier flight with the last load, I received a request on the radio for one more flight. Upon returning to Talkeetna, I was given instructions to perform a back haul out of the west fork of the Ruth Glacier. I was to fly in with the Super Cub to pick up Charlie Porter's heavy ice-covered gear, the last remains of the survival site. Mike and Jim appointed me, rationalizing that because I was lighter than the other pilots, I would be able to take more gear in the plane.

Mike Fisher gave me a map, which he hastily scrawled on a wrinkled paper bag which was previously inhabited by his lunch. The map warned me away from the site on the glacier where he had landed and had become stuck. Fisher suggested a safer landing spot. His sketch marked a crater where the first plane had been buried, the landing tracks, the location of the stashed gear and noted some crevasses and other hazards to avoid. He left me with one warning: that I needed to hurry because the weather was deteriorating and time was limited.

I took off in changing weather and the increasingly flat light of the Alaskan summer afternoons. Flying up through the Ruth Gorge and past the Sheldon Amphitheater, I circled above the West Fork of the glacier. As I did this, I attempted to use Fisher's landing map, but the drawing just didn't feel right. The area was completely shadowed, which complicated my depth perception. Next to where the map recommended I land was a double fall line caused by sliding side ridges merging with the glacier. This created two side cuts and could mean an uneven landing surface that might lead to stubbing a ski and flipping the Cub. It was crucial to choose an area that avoided crevasses to allow myself enough room to land and turn the Cub around to be in position to fly out. I was acutely aware of the fuel quantity, the rate of consumption and the threat posed by a thick mass of nasty weather creeping up the glacier with dense clouds hovering in the valley below.

I decided that with these risks, landing on Mike's former landing ski tracks bordered by crevasses was necessary, though he had cautioned otherwise. I set the Cub up for landing and touched down on the glacier, stopping short of the large hole created by the C185. I pushed a bit of power to turn the plane around in the new snow, facing the direction for takeoff.

Climbing out of the airplane, I glanced at the hole just a few feet away. It was wider and deeper than I'd thought, confirming the difficulty of trying to read a surface from altitude in the flat light and snow conditions. I saw a few pink wands identifying Porter's cache about 100 feet away. I also saw exposed crevasses and estimated that there were twice as many that were not visible.

XXVI

I uneasily walked the distance to Porter's orange plastic sled, into which I could load his gear along with an icy climbing rope, which I took back to the plane to use as a safety line. I knotted one end of the rope to my belt and the other to the aircraft strut and then trudged through the deep snow to move the remaining loads of gear into the plane. The gear was heavy but I managed to lug it all, laughing at how strange it was to be completely alone on a glacier and the absurdity of tying myself to a rope, which provided more of a false sense of security than anything else.

As I was packing the final load of Porter's cache onto the sled, a thunderous sound reverberated across the landscape. I looked up to face a churning river of snow boiling down the steep mountainside toward me. A massive avalanche had cut loose and was spilling off Mt. Huntington, and I was standing directly in its path.

I turned from the sled and quickly checked to ensure that the rope - my lifeline - was taut. The Hail Mary prayer flashed into my head. I thought, here I was, a girl from Chicago now standing before a charging avalanche on a remote glacier in the middle of Alaska! I stomped my feet into the snow to brace for the impact and waited for the inevitable. Seconds later, the Cub disappeared, cocooned in a cloud of frigid, whirling snow. A rush of whiteness enveloped my plane and me. Unable to see anything, I waited for it to pass in a moment that seemed to last forever.

Then, as suddenly as the thundering wall of snow had started, it stopped. The vibrations beneath my feet ceased. I was surrounded by an eerie silence. I realized that I had been holding my breath and began to gulp the thin air. When the mist settled, the Super Cub remained, covered in white but untouched. Miraculously, the avalanche stopped just meters short of us.

Sound was hauntingly muted and the dry crunch of my boots echoed within the strange acoustics created by the new layer of snow. I pulled my rope from its shallow snow cover and kept it tight as I moved toward the plane. I tugged at the door release, hoping the door wasn't frozen shut, and was relieved that it opened for me to reach for the small shovel that was part of my survival gear. I dug out the Cub's buried skis and then with the rope, I cleared as much snow from the Cub's wings as I could, knowing that avalanches can trigger further activity.

I loaded the frozen cargo and climbed in. Mixture, master, mags, and I pushed the starter. The engine coughed once and the sound of the rpm drone was like music to me. After a quick run up and a spin of the stick to check the controls, I adjusted the mixture, pushed the throttle to full and the plane grudgingly gained speed through the new snow and clawed its way up into the thin air. I needed enough altitude to get above Mt. Huntington's 10,500-foot mass and above the thick ceiling of clouds now rolling up the glacier.

Walls of granite and ice surrounded me and there was very little room in which to maneuver. My fuel was low since I had needed the plane to be as light as possible to accommodate the heavy gear. Circling, I coaxed the Cub to gain altitude. In my third climbing circle, I radioed the TAT office to give a position report and climbed above the thick cloud cover into scattered bits of clear sky.

Kitty on top in Cub during glacier rescue

Once on top, I turned south to head back to Talkeetna. After landing at the state airstrip, taxiing in and shutting down the plane, I patted the Cub's panel and said a thankful prayer with a smile. I was relieved and more than exhausted but I was also exhilarated and proud to have completed the job. Jim and Mike would later joke, "Glad you got it all. We didn't want to go back up there ourselves! We're fresh out of lemon drops."

Jim Banner & Kitty

CHAPTER ONE

Childhood

"A thinker recognizes the sovereign control of her own mind and... thinks for herself, considers the evidence, seeks the truth, and builds her life upon it... The thinker creates ideas with humility knowing that behind the idea that she calls her own are the thoughts and efforts of many... She strives to develop a mature mind without losing the simplicity of childhood."

—Peterson

The summer she was 14 years old, Kitty Banner was belted into the right front seat of a Beechcraft V-tail Bonanza heading to northern Wisconsin from Chicago. She was seated next to her brother, Denny, ten years her senior and a pilot. She watched his every move, fascinated by his detail and hanging onto his explanations as if, for her benefit, he read his checklist aloud. She heard the engine catch and settle into a low growl and Denny's right arm stretched across her lap to lock the door with a firm snap. The taxi completed and the run-up performed, the aircraft surged along the runway, reached upward, lifted off and headed north.

They were bound for the family summer cottage in Three Lakes, Wisconsin, and her heart pulsed with the rhythm of the engine. Glancing back over her shoulder at Lake Michigan, she watched whitecaps crest and roll. Ahead and growing larger as they neared, Milwaukee clung to the lakeshore. To avoid airborne traffic arriving and departing from the city's airport, Denny veered slightly to the west-northwest. Kitty rocked gently with fluid motions of the airplane, watching the wing rise as Denny banked and then subtlety returned to level flight.

Soon, fields below became a vast feather quilt, a living comforter of brown, green, red and yellow crisscrossed with blue rivers and dotted with even bluer ponds. Up ahead, Winnebago, one of Wisconsin's largest lakes, painted a swath of vibrant blue amid the agricultural fields and Green Bay's beautiful Door Peninsula. Denny weaved their aircraft around the cumulus clouds. Bits and pieces of reflected light danced throughout the cockpit and Kitty pretended she was parachuting out to bounce from one puffy cloud to another. Freedom, power, elegance and control. That's what flying felt like to Kitty.

Catherine "Kitty" Banner was born on the first of September in 1952 to Jack and Helen Banner of Chicago, Illinois. She was the fourth child and the first girl to follow three older brothers. Several years later, a fifth child, Kitty's sister, Ginny, was born. The family was part of a close-knit community of congregants of the Queen of All Saints Parish, and was equally close to their neighbors in the Sauganash and Lincolnwood areas of the north side of Chicago.

The Banners loved to entertain. They hosted dinner parties and would sing and dance to tunes on the piano for hours. Along with friends, they bought a lake cottage in the North Woods of Three Lakes, Wisconsin. Joy and laughter reverberated from the walls of their home, and like the strong inviting aromas of a bubbling Irish stew, music, sports, adventure, camaraderie and creativity surrounded the Banners. It was a time of economic prosperity and Banner's third-generation, century-old business, Thomas B. Banner Boiler and Construction, prospered during those years. The company had a deep history in marine business on the Great Lakes and installed commercial heating systems in famed buildings such as Chicago's Sears Tower, now named Willis Tower.

Jack Banner had an uncharacteristic generosity since the days of his youth. Jack had been imbued with a deep appreciation for the good works of the Sisters of Charity, the religious community of women who through teaching and serving the poor in schools and orphanages, spread kindness across the United States - including taking a large role in helping raise his mother and aunt.

Kitty's great grandmother, Mary McDermott Shannon, a young 17-year-old had travelled by ship alone from Galway, Ireland to the United States.

McDermott met the handsome and gregarious Mike Shannon – charming but unreliable. They moved to Chicago where Mary separated from Shannon to raise her daughters on her own – a radical move for an Irish Catholic woman in those days. As a single parent Mary struggled to work full time to support Jack's mother, Kitty Shannon and her sister, Margaret Shannon. The Sisters of Saint Vincent DePaul would watch the two girls while their mother worked.

Jack's father had enjoyed a comfortable upbringing and inheritance of the family business. Because of extensive background in the boiler business in Chicago, a trade that originated from making repairs on ships, Jack enlisted in the Navy in 1942. He returned to Chicago after the war, where he took over the family business and with Helen, dedicated a lifetime of support to the work of the St. Vincent de Paul Center in downtown Chicago. They would share this charitable attitude with their children, giving them a heritage of generosity. Yearly, her father would suggest that each child choose a useful and special garment of theirs to donate to children being cared for by St. Vincent de Paul. At eight years old, Kitty remembered reluctantly picking her favorite winter coat. She held the warm coat against her lap as they drove to the center. Hoping to drop the coat into one of the bins outside, they instead went in to deliver it personally. To her surprise, when she attempted to give it to the waiting nun, the Sister smiled gently, shook her head, and said, "We'd like you to take it to the girl who is to receive it."

Her father drove to the address they had been given and sent Kitty up the walk to the tenement apartment. Peeling paint, a broken bicycle, debris in the entryway and a hole in the screen door spoke volumes, but she was most impressed with the eyes of the girl who answered her knock at that door, a girl exactly her height but with eyes devoid of the sparkle Kitty's couldn't hide. She held out the coat and watched a slow, sad smile creep across the girl's face as she reached for it, dropped her gaze, and murmured, "Thank you."

The lesson lingered, just one of many never to be forgotten. It influenced who Kitty would become and strengthened her growing awareness that happiness wasn't to be pursued; it comes from involvement and kindness with others. She was learning that happiness depended upon her own spirit and would result from her behaviors and choices.

Like their father, who spent his early years as an athlete and lifeguard on the shores of Lake Michigan, Dennis, Jim, and John, her older brothers, were accomplished in many sports, but perhaps most importantly, flying. Kitty and Ginny emulated their older brothers closely, who in turn, included them in their adventures without altering their expectations or making allowances for the fact that they were girls.

Jim, seven years older than Kitty, enjoyed competitive archery and handgun target practice and would often invite Kitty to come shooting with him. Ginny had a vivacious spirit developed through a talent for horseback riding, which she shared with Jim. She rode Western and English saddles and excelled in showmanship. Kitty would ride Ginny's Quarter horse but avoided her feisty Thoroughbred, named Brian Boru after a King of Ireland. Kitty would say to Ginny, "You're into horses; I'm into horsepower."

The Banner's family home was located near the home of a District Attorney serving in 1968-1969. He was presiding over the highly-publicized trial of the Chicago Seven, who were accused of plotting to incite a riot to interrupt Chicago's 1968 Democratic National Convention.

Douglas Linder, a law professor at the University of Missouri, was featured in papers stating, "Culturally and politically, 1968 was one of the most turbulent years ever in America. *Hair*, a controversial new musical about draftees and flower children, introduced frontal nudity. Feminists picketed the Miss America pageant. Black students demanded Black Studies programs and Eldridge Cleaver published *Soul on Ice*."

Kitty was a junior in high school with her brand-new driver's license. A friend called asking for her help in getting drivers to transport speakers, including actors like Jane Fonda, Dennis Hopper and cast members from *Hair*, to the Vietnam moratorium going on at the Playboy Mansion during the Chicago Seven trial.

As Kitty approached the mansion, she saw a long line of women all linked arm and arm. They were a faction of the Women's Movement. "Burn your Bra" was one of their many slogans. She had to break the women's picket line as they were attempting to bar anyone from entry to the mansion. As she pushed her way through, a reporter approached her, thrusting a microphone in her face and demanding, "How do you feel as a woman, breaking the Women's Movement picket line?"

Kitty responded, "I'm an independent person with independent thoughts. I believe in the Women's Movement, but right now the Vietnam moratorium is more important to me."

She was then led through, accompanied by police. That particular event would come to represent a path of independence throughout her life.

During this time, Kitty's brother, Jim, served as foreman for Banner Boiler. Once while Jack was out of town, Kitty coaxed Jim into hiring her to drive a company truck. She always wanted to work for dad's company and jumped at the chance to learn welding and truck driving. He gave her some lessons, along with warnings about the locations into which she would go and cautioned, "When you are driving a truck in any large city, you have to be wary of the back alleys and locations where you can get stuck. There are nasty places you don't want to go, especially deliveries in secluded work sites. Never pin yourself in. Always leave the truck in a position that allows you to floor it and get out!"

When her father returned to Chicago and saw that Kitty was learning arc welding and truck driving, he put a stop to both immediately. He not only thought it wasn't appropriate, he knew from experience that both could be dangerous. Knowing that Kitty's enthusiasm far outweighed her skills and that she could accidentally blow up the building while practicing welding, he transferred her into the office.

Kitty's love and appreciation for flying came from her brothers, three men she most admired. Denny, who saw service in the U.S. Navy, used his benefits under the G.I. Bill in 1966 to obtain a private pilot certificate. He served in sales for *The New Yorker* magazine and used a Beech Bonanza to cover his sales territory. Later, as Vice President of Corporate Sales for CBS Publishing, he used aircraft to vastly expand his reach. Eventually, his passion for flight took him from publishing to a highly successful private aviation career, Banner Aviation, based in Waukegan, Illinois. Denny has accrued more than 12,000 hours as pilot in command. His wife, Susan, received her private pilot certificate in 1973. Together, Denny and Susan owned more than 40 different jets and turboprop aircraft. He has flown numerous celebrity clients and guided many through the complicated business of aircraft ownership.

John, three years older than Kitty, and with a wide variety of interests, is a corporate pilot who has circled the globe. A mountain climber, he learned to sleep while hanging suspended in hammocks on sheer wall faces. Together, he, Kitty, and Kitty's friend, Nancy, traveled in Ireland, exploring the countryside of the British Isles. John left them in Ireland and went to the Himalayas. Kitty, green with envy, found out that he was there, climbing to the base camp on Mt. Everest at 18,000 feet with an Italian expedition. There he met missionaries representing the Moody Bible Institute. Much later and in entirely different circumstances, Kitty would meet the same missionary pilots in Bellingham, Washington. John would always say to Kitty, "You can come along if you can pack your own bag, carry your own freight, and pay your own way."

Kitty's older brothers were protective, but they instilled reality with the spirit of adventure.

Denny Banner, Banner Aviation

Denny Banner:
THE AIRPLANE GUY

QUEEN OF ALL
SAINTS 1958-59

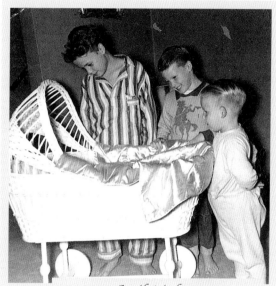

A pilot is born

Jack Banner Banner Boiler & Construction

Banner Boiler has a rich, interesting history. In the 1920s it was located on Austin Avenue (now Hubbard St.) and Thomas Banner at one time even owned several sightseeing boats. Jack Banner, today's president, is shown in front of the firm's office on North Kedzie. See story on Page 4.

Kitty Banner High School
Senior Picture, 1970

John, Denny, Jim, Kitty, Ginny,
Laurell with Midgie & Spirit

Thunder & Ginny Banner

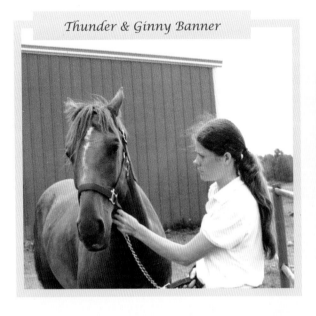

Susan Banner & Sunny
with C-210

Banner home in Sauganash, Illinois

Jack Banner

Denny, Jim, & John at Jim's wedding

John Banner flying Cataract Canyon in C210

John Corsini, Laura Fisher, Nancy Kelly,
Kitty, Frank Thompson at Regis College

CHAPTER TWO

Traveling

"Travel patiently. It takes time to understand others, especially when there are barriers of language and custom; keep flexible and adaptable to all situations."

—Peterson

Nobody called it "dating" in the 1960s and 1970s. At colleges across the United States, students hung out together and relationships were comfortably fluid, loose and uncommitted.

Kitty was drawn to the alma mater of her three older brothers, Regis College, a private Jesuit liberal arts school in Denver, Colorado. Trail hiking, skiing, and fishing all enhanced the location. The freshman orientation included a camping trip in the mountains. The dramatic white-capped peaks and demanding, rugged hiking trails took a little acclimating and Kitty found it exhilarating.

Regis was sufficiently far enough from Chicago to give Kitty a healthy dose of independence. Her freshman year was filled with new challenges and experiences. For the first time in her life, Kitty experienced homesickness. She called home and Jim answered. Her parents were out of town and after a short discussion he said, "Go to Stapleton Airport. A ticket will be waiting for you."

He met her at the Chicago O'Hare Airport and brought her up to date. Everything was as it had been, an affirmation that home was still there. Kitty stayed for two nights before returning to Regis, but homesickness never clawed at her with that kind of power again. She embraced familial love, her valuable and sustaining Irish blessing.

Kitty enjoyed both years at Regis, yet wondered about attending a larger school which could offer new opportunities. As a self-described Virgo, she made a list of dreams, plans and goals. That summer, she visited Chicago's Old Town and got together for dinner with Bill Murray, a friend from high school and Regis who had recently returned from a trip. He told Kitty that he caught a ride hitchhiking from Canada with a professor from Western Washington State College in Bellingham. They became friends and he stayed with him for weeks to help build his log cabin. He was so impressed with the college and its environs, he recommended it to Kitty. That year, she and life-long

Bill Murray, Mary Rothermich, John Lafferty, Mary "Murf" Murphy, Kitty, & Sarah Schwaba

friend, Nancy Kelly, submitted their applications to Western Washington. The school would come to change her life and Kitty would be forever grateful to Murray for this advice.

Murray's adventure had sparked Kitty's desire to travel. At the end of her sophomore year, she took a semester off and visited Alaska for the first time. She was nineteen. With a friend, John Lafferty, and his Doberman, they set out in his Toyota FJ40 Land Cruiser. They drove from Tulsa, Oklahoma, to Bellingham, Washington, and hopped a small ferry, the *TAKU*, to Juneau.

The ship made stops and they explored the fertile, tree-lined ports of Alaska's Inside Passage. The area was rich with marine life. Whales abundantly graced the bays and extraordinary flocks of birds migrated through everything - the air, trees, land and water.

Ketchikan and Sitka were lined with towering majestic totem poles. The trip was also the first time Kitty saw the Mendenhall Glacier. Located just outside of Juneau, it was a remnant of the last ice age on the North American continent. It was an adventure that celebrated the coastal beauty of the last frontier. She realized that she liked the rugged surroundings and sought to make them her own.

Kitty was not finished traveling before transferring to her next university. Along with Nancy, they had a strong desire to visit their birthright country, Ireland, and learn about their personal family histories that connected them to the British Isles. Kitty Shannon Murphy Banner, Kitty's self-styled Irish name, honors both her paternal namesake, grandmother Kitty Shannon, as well as maternal namesake, aunt Kitty Murphy. Eager to explore their roots and investigate the programs and degrees offered by a modern European college, the two set off for Trinity College in Dublin to visit the Book of Kells gallery, Ireland's greatest cultural treasure and world's most famous medieval manuscript.

It was 1972 and a tense time in Ireland. The girls arrived at Shannon Airport just one day ahead of a bomb explosion in one of the terminal buildings. While on a weekend trip to London, they were stunned to hear that a bomb had been defused at Harrods, located in Knightsbridge, just a day after they visited there.

Kitty and Nancy pressed on, traveling from one hostel to another and finding rooms at university dormitories. One night, they went to a pub to hear Séamus Ennis play his fiddle and Uilleann Pipes. Ennis was a famous folklore and music collector with an amazing ability to speak and understand a wide variety of regional Gaelic dialects. He was a living treasure trove of music that otherwise would have been lost to history. Also on the bill was the accordionist Paddy O'Brien, who at the time was just a few years older than Kitty and Nancy. He played jigs, reels, hornpipes, airs, marches and some rare Irish tunes. A bomb went off days after that show at the same Dublin pub.

"It's so full of tension here," Kitty wrote to her parents.

While in Ireland, Kitty and Nancy learned they were accepted at Western Washington State College. Reinvigorated and wizened by their recent travels, they returned to Chicago and moved to Bellingham. Lummi Island was immediately to the west and the cluster of cedar-studded San Juan Islands lay beyond. On misty mornings, the islands seemed to rise from their indigo waters of the Straits of Juan de Fuca and Georgia, an inspiration for landscape artists to capture their elusive beauty on canvases.

Complementing the marine views were spectacular landforms to the east, dominated by majestic Mt. Baker, a 10,741-foot dormant volcano, one of the many historical volcanoes that have come to form The Ring of Fire. The very names – Mts. Rainier, St. Helens, Adams, Hood, Jefferson, Bachelor, Three Sisters, Mazama, Shasta and Lassen – evoke images of glorious peaks that stud the Cascade Mountains from Canada to California; rugged, craggy, solitary giants capped in white mantles of snow and ice lying in wait of their next explosive seismic shudders. Kitty had yet to experience the lofty, silent and icy Mt. Baker, famed for being the site of one of the greatest snow packs in the continental United States and crowning jewel of the Northern Cascades. Little did Kitty know how majestically this mountain would reign over coming adventures, and it would all begin in a small city near its foothills.

Dave Rahm's Bücker Jungmann near Mt. Rainier

CHAPTER THREE

Friendship

"To be a friend, one should start by being a friend to one's own self; by being true to one's own highest and best...."

—Peterson

"It was like being in a painting," Kitty wrote in her diary, describing her first days taking in the grandeur of her new surroundings. She and Nancy felt so small surrounded by such tall trees, giant mountains and a huge body of water. After a semester living in an apartment on campus, they rented an old Victorian house in downtown Bellingham.

During enrollment, Kitty signed up for an Irish History class taught by Giovanni Costigan, a specialist in Irish and English history. Costigan, born in 1905 to Irish parents in Kingston-on-Thames, England, and educated at Oxford, taught a seminal course in the University of Washington system from 1934 to 1975. Kitty was thrilled to experience the eloquence and drama of Costigan's legendary lectures. In one of these Irish History classes, Kitty met Stephanie Forrest, a brilliant student and strong female athlete who soon became one of Kitty's good friends. Stephanie competed on the U.S. Ski Team and excelled as a parachutist and horsewoman. Eventually, she would earn a doctorate in Computer and Communication Sciences from the

University of Michigan and gain renown as a professor and chairman of computer science at the University of New Mexico. Kitty was intrigued one day by Stephanie's casual mention of heading out to Bellingham's small airport where she worked in the office at the Fixed Base Operation (FBO). It turned out that one of her passions was parachute jumping.

Kitty & Stephanie

Stephanie, then a member of the U.S. Parachute Team, introduced Kitty to Ken, the jumpmaster at the Blaine Airstrip located right on the border with Canada. In a short time, Kitty made her first parachute jump.

Kitty discovered what it felt like to climb to altitude and leap. They went to the drop zone the night before the planned jump and Ken put Kitty through the training. The next day, as the airplane began its ascent to 3,200 feet, Kitty was exhilarated, soaring above and surrounded with natural beauty in every direction. That experience in the plane, even before the jump, resonated deeply with her. She knew she wanted to learn to fly.

Admittedly, the thought of jumping through the opened door had her heart beating and her hands damp with sweat. She followed the steps of Ken's training and Kitty positioned herself in front of the open door. She reached for the strut bracing the wing to the airplane body and secured her foot on the step, all while fighting the slipstream and prop wash. She felt the expected slap on the thigh they'd promised when they could see she was properly positioned to release her grip. She took in a big breath and then looked down at the ground far below her 3,200 feet above the earth.

They had warned her that if she failed to arch her body she would tumble. Ken had also said that the canopy would open eight seconds after she jumped. She tightened her back into an arch, spread her arms, and started to count, "One thousand, two thousand, three thousand..."

It was breathtaking. It was awesome. Her body had truly taken flight. She kept counting. At six, the static line opened the parachute with a sharp tug. She glanced up, but the oversized borrowed helmet she had on slid down over her eyes and nose. Pushing it up, she saw her chute was fully opened and properly billowed.

The view, as she floated toward the ground, was spectacular. She could see the Canadian Mountains, Cascade Mountain Range, Olympic Peninsula and the San Juan Islands strung like glowing jade gems laid across the Straits of Juan de Fuca. Down below, a fluorescent orange tarp marked the drop zone. She had been instructed to pull the appropriate toggle to steer left or right for a good landing. After the figurative "plunge into her future," Kitty took an introductory flight in a Cessna 150 at Bellingham Airport and loved it. That same evening, she told Nancy that she was going to learn to fly.

Kitty's next challenge was to choose a major course of study. Having renewed the joy triggered by flying, she was eager to focus on her new and consuming career objective – aviation. Nancy suggested she pursue a degree combining aviation with liberal arts through Fairhaven College of Interdisciplinary Studies at Western Washington State College, now Western Washington University.

Kitty realized that to continue covering her college tuition, she needed to land a job that could finance her flying lessons. She was hired at the Bellingham Airport's local FBO, fueling local and transient aircraft. In short, she was the "Little Gas Gal". Her job offered her a salary as well as access and discounts to rental aircraft. The job's official description on her résumé became "Chief Fuel Dispersal Technician, Bellingham International Airport."

Kitty lived on Lake Samish, which was close enough to the Bellingham Airport to respond to calls at all hours of the night and early morning to keep pilots promptly and properly refueled so they could be off again. She quickly discovered that many of the planes coming through were traveling to the Experimental Aircraft Association's series of annual fly-ins like those held in Oshkosh, Wisconsin. Such aerial conventions drew an eclectic series of aircraft and the parade of homebuilt aircraft never ceased to intrigue Kitty and provided her chances to meet a host of do-it-yourselfers who built aircraft from kits with loving attention to detail obvious in their completed works.

On January 8, 1974, Kitty logged her initial flight with Dave Rahm, flight instructor, aerobatic air show performer, geology professor and the owner and pilot of a Bücker Jungmann, a single-seat Pitts Special and a Cessna 180. His command of the machines raised flying from a challenging athletic endeavor to an art form. He introduced her to geomorphology, which enhanced the entire project. Beyond that, he helped Kitty arrange her dual major in two simultaneous courses of study.

Rahm swore by the acronym PEDPERS: Presentation, Explanation, Demonstration, Practice, Evaluation and Repetition. He wasn't alone. Scores of flight instructors accepted this standardized method for introducing new students to flight. In many cases, a student could expect his introduction to flight to include a pre-flight walk-around, familiarization with the controls, descriptions of the three axes of flight: pitch, yaw, and roll, hands-on duplication of an instructor's demonstrations of flight basics: straight and level, climbs, turns, descents and a follow-through to a demonstrated landing. Aerial maneuvers at the hands of Rahm were a breathtaking exploration of air, space and mechanical wizardry. Kitty's flight lessons were startling departures from the mundane. She learned to fly as if the machine and pilot were one.

Pulitzer-Prize winning author, Annie Dillard, also flew with Rahm. Awed by his prowess in an air show, she wrote in *The Writing Life*: "Rahm did everything his plane could do: tailspins, four-point rolls, flat spins, figure eights, snap rolls and hammerheads. He did pirouettes on the plane's tail. The other pilots could do these stunts, too, skillfully, one at a time. But Rahm used the plane inexhaustibly, like a brush marking thin air. His was pure energy and naked spirit. He made beauty with his whole body."

As a geologist, he was intensely interested in all landforms. He reveled in studying the highest peaks to the deepest canyons. If something caught his attention, he'd spontaneously roll into a dive to better view dry creek beds, glacial cirques, granite outcroppings, crevasses, ridges and rivers. He'd turn nature's shapes into reference points for maneuvering close to the ground, defying gravity, ensuring that every flight was a celebration of the natural and mechanical world. After only a second flight with Rahm, Kitty's logbook noted: "Use of controls, medium bank turns, power off stalls, slow flight, power on stalls, stall recoveries, turns following a river and spins."

In turns following the river, they were down just off the deck. Like the water that lapped at their wheels, their airplane flowed with a sweeping bank to the right, followed immediately with a smooth, steep reverse to the left. His hand on the yoke and his feet tapping the rudder pedals transferred his smooth, subtle corrections to fluid motion. His every move was an inspiration. Kitty wanted to fly just like he flew. In a little over two weeks, eight hours and 23 minutes in the air, Rahm approved Kitty for her first supervised solo flight. Yet again, it proved to be a departure from a common practice of expecting a new solo student pilot to perform two touch-and-goes with a third landing to a complete stop. She did the requisite touch-and-goes. But rather than coming to a full stop, she left the traffic pattern and flew to the practice area where she performed steep turns and went through some power-on and power-off stalls, exploring her own piece of sky. Without her instructor's weight, it was a brand-new experience, a new airplane. Kitty was ecstatic to be alone, to feel the control pressures that reflected changes in weight and balance, to glance to her right and see no one there. She was free, in control, and loved every moment of it.

Rahm signed her off to perform supervised solo cross-country flights and each became an exploration of self as well as machine. She couldn't imagine a more magical area to learn to fly. On her first solo flight to Boeing Field, Mt. Rainier was stately and bare. No clouds masked its beauty and it evoked a deserving awe as it loomed just to the southeast. She also knew she would be landing on an airport that was one of the nation's busiest, with more than 300,000 takeoffs and landings a year. It was thrilling.

Kitty flew a dual cross-country east of the Cascades to Ellensburg with her instructor Rahm. She was entranced by seemingly endless stands of the evergreens, aspen and cottonwoods of Snoqualmie National Forest. They flew above the highway that snaked through Stevens Pass among the peaks of the snow-covered Wenatchee Mountains then descended into the high desert region of eastern Washington with its mighty Columbia River and verdant fruit orchards of Yakima Valley bordering the Wenatchee River passing over Alpine Falls. They landed to take on fuel at Ellensburg's Bowers Field and departed for the return flight which followed Interstate 90, the major road connecting Spokane and Seattle.

Kitty made note of two airports. One of them, the municipal airport at Cle Elum, hugged Interstate 90 between the Yakima River and the pristine jewel of a lake that bore its name. Another, in Easton, Washington, and on the path to Snoqualmie Pass renowned for its glorious Snoqualmie Falls, was the state airport serving Easton and Roslyn, Washington. She paid only limited interest to Roslyn and the grass strip which looked like a postage stamp, noting it as a haven or a port in a storm should anything require her to divert from a future flight plan. The airfield at Roslyn was constructed in the 1930s as an emergency field for DC-3s crossing the Cascades through Snoqualmie Pass. Its grass runway was 2,640 feet in length with a 300-foot displaced threshold on the west end. She noted the trees surrounding the airport and recognized them as obstacles to both approach ends of the runway. The notices also called attention to the fact that "deer, elk and motorcyclists also enjoy the airport and its surface is somewhat rough. As it will be soft when wet, it was recommended that pre-landing over flight be performed to check field and obstructions. The airport is generally open from the first of June to the first of October and, with a field elevation of 2,221 feet, density altitude problems can be encountered in the summer."

Just barely a solo pilot that day, years would pass before Roslyn and its little dirt strip would be significant in her life. That dual cross-country to Ellensburg was only the tip of an iceberg of knowledge and skills she acquired from Rahm and others over years of hard work and practice.

While Kitty was gaining flight time and progressing with her skills at the controls of an airplane, she was working to gain approval from the Western Washington's Board of Directors for her unconventional double major. She spent weeks researching the curricula of the liberal arts and aviation classes. She wanted to connect the study of aviation with geomorphology, including aerial cartography and photography. Her aim was to merge the technical study of aviation with the liberal arts. Rahm thought that the interdisciplinary combination of liberal arts and technology could be a distinct advantage to the serious student.

With several pushes, the Board of Directors finally allowed the combination degree. In this world of her own making, she profited by achieving a solid liberal arts background while simultaneously accruing flight experience. She was even given the opportunities to fly with geologists who pursued aerial photography and earth science study made possible through aviation.

When it came time for her to work toward her flight test and log the requisite experience, Kitty was signed off for her first solo cross-country to Toledo, Oregon where she obtained the obligatory signatures in her log book, a 600-mile round trip. The flight would be a much longer distance than the normal required 300 miles with a touch-and-go on return at Paine Field, also known as Snohomish County Airport and Bayview. A solo cross-country is a special event for any new pilot but as she flew over the gorgeous waters, cedars, shorelines and passed islands to the west, Kitty's experience was beyond routine.

Dave Rahm lent some singular purpose to another dual cross-country flight. In 1973, Rahm had suffered an engine failure in his Bücker Jungmann. He was performing in an air show on the east side of the Cascade Range and lost the engine when en route to Bellingham over rugged terrain.

Unable to restart the engine, he had to suffer a crash landing. Fortunately, Rahm wasn't badly hurt. The tail of his biplane was tattered, its wings badly damaged and the fuselage torn. Arrangements were made for the craft to be picked up, repaired and restored by Hobart Sorrell and his sons John, Mark and Tim of Sorrell Aviation in Tenino, Washington.

He suggested that Kitty flight-plan a dual cross-country flight to Tenino to check on the progress of the Bücker Jungmann. Flight students are generally assigned to plan an initial flight to a distant destination airport for a demonstration of cross-country flight planning and techniques. This involved a much more challenging departure. Kitty and Rahm planned a six-hour round-robin flight between Bellingham, Port Angeles, Ocean Shores, Moquiam, the Flying B, Tacoma, Paine and Tenino with return to Bellingham. Included was the required plotting of omni navigation, dead reckoning, weather analysis and adherence to pertinent Visual Flight Rules (VFR). Kitty was to plan a flight encompassing almost the entire measurement of the state, from its northernmost border with Canada to the Columbia River, the dividing line between Washington and Oregon.

Her logbook simply noted a "Dual flight in a Cessna 150 on February 7, 1974, from Bellingham (BLI) to Tenino and the Sorrell's grass field."

In reality, Kitty's first extended departure from her familiar home airport included mountain flying, air traffic to see and avoid, position reports to be radioed, unpredictable wintry weather conditions and myriad details that make cross-country flying a mixture of mystery and challenge. She performed well and more than justified his belief in her abilities. The long, busy flight would include her first grass-field landing, and after a successful conclusion, she satisfied the requirements well enough that Rahm approved her to pilot the route as solo.

Several weeks later, Rahm had Kitty repeat the three-hour cross-country to pick up his airplane. On the return to Bellingham, Kitty was solo in the Cessna, maintaining loose formation with Rahm's biplane-no mean feat. Formation flying, even for two aircraft in loose trail, demands skill levels that generally require interdependency and experience. Close formation requires a strict division of attention between one's own craft and that of another, and a high level of mutual confidence. Even loose formation can be distracting and demanding. Despite her instructor flying her wing, or perhaps because of an instructor flying her wing, a student pilot might have blanched at soloing a Cessna 150 in formation for three hours through the most populated section of Washington State.

The Seattle area is also a beehive of aerial activity, a heavily-used corridor for air traffic between the Orient, Alaska, Canada and the United States. It is home to Paine Field in Everett, Boeing Field (King County International Airport), Seattle-Tacoma International Airport, McChord Air Force Base, Fort Lewis Military Reservation and a corridor narrowed topographically because of the ocean, Puget Sound, Olympic Mountains to the west and rapidly rising terrain to the east.

Their distracting beauties aside, the northern Cascade Mountains form a classic chain like a skeletal spinal column. Its peaks, from Mt. Baker at 10,778 feet, Mt. Daniel at 7,986 feet, to Mt. Snoqualmie at 4,176 feet, are sentinels guarding the foothills and serve to direct a pilot's respectful awe to the powerful and breathtaking 14,411 foot Mt. Rainier. Pilots who fly in these environs can never take them for granted. Mountain pilots sometimes learn the hard way the hazards of wind, updrafts, downdrafts, circling eddies and in the Cascades, the unpredictable Chinook foehn winds that are rivaled only by California's Santa Anas.

Rahm radioed to keep her aircraft straight and level while he performed a barrel roll around the Cessna. They took their cameras along on that cross-country flight. Kitty used Rahm's Rolleiflex to take pictures of him off her wing with Mt. Rainier in the background and Lake Washington below. He later sent her an enlargement of that photo, which to this day hangs on the wall in her home.

Dave Rahm, Bücker Jungmann in Washington

CHAPTER FOUR

Work

To log flying time, Kitty took every flight opportunity that came along. Every flight was a new experience and every landing at a formerly unknown field contributed confidence that she might not have gained any other way. She was asked to deliver a Cessna 150 for radio repair to Boeing Field. With the radio out, she had to call ahead, plan her arrival time carefully and wait for the green light from the tower controller to legally land. Dave Rahm recommended Kitty for her private pilot flight test on May 5, 1974, and five days later she earned her certificate as a private pilot. Shortly after, Rahm gave her instruction in his Bücker.

"The right attitude toward work multiplies achievement. [The art of work] is idealizing your work, turning a job into a mission, a task into a career."
—Peterson

Rahm's Pitts was a small single seat biplane, but he did give Kitty dual in his Cessna 180 taildragger and gave her additional instruction in a Piper Cub. "Loved it! Cub flying is fun!" Kitty wrote in her diary. But it was Rahm's German open cockpit biplane that left an indelible mark. Kitty would always remember watching Mt. Baker erupting on one spectacular flight. It was sunset and the mountain was steaming. Just as the whites of the smoke were spun into the reds of the sunset, Rahm rolled inverted and they were upside down, hanging from their shoulder straps, gazing inside the active volcano.

Not every new experience was aerial, though. One day, Kitty went canoeing with Stephanie Forrest. As they checked crab pots along the shoreline near her home, Stephanie mentioned that her brother, Kimball, was arriving from Hawaii. Kitty asked how Kimball was going to get to Bellingham and when Stephanie answered that she was picking him up, Kitty offered to drive her in her Datsun pickup. Little did she know that the exceptionally talented man she was about to meet was destined to make a huge difference in her life.

On their route back from the airport, Kimball asked her, "So, you're a pilot?"

"I am," Kitty told him. "I just got my certificate. I'm working out at the airport."

Kimball said, "Really? I work there. What do you do?"

"I'm the fuel attendant," she said.

He responded, "That's my job."

"Not any longer," Kitty retorted with a smile. She added, "I especially like meeting pilots flying through from Alaska. Their stories make me want to be a part of the whole Alaska scene."

Later, Kitty was at Stephanie and Kimball's family home in the Chuckanut Mountains, a short bike ride south of Bellingham, when Stephanie asked for another ride to the airport to catch a flight to Hawaii. Kitty spoke up and said, "I'll take you to Sea-Tac in the Cessna 150."

Stephanie woke Kimball and told him that Kitty had offered to fly her into Seattle's International Airport. Kitty had never flown in there before and Kimball knew she was pretty green. His comment was, "Well, you've got to get your feet wet sometime."

That was all the encouragement Kitty needed. Stephanie and Kitty flew down, landed Sea-Tac, and started taxiing. Kitty was monitoring ground control when the controller asked, "Where are you going?"

Bellingham Airport, Kitty (the gas gal) & Lori, 1974

Kitty keyed the mic and replied that her passenger was flying out on a flight and she was going to taxi to the United gates to catch her aircraft.

"Um, no, that's not how it works," the controller replied.

She was directed to an air taxi area where passengers in private aircraft were to be dropped off. All part of the learning curve.

Not long after, Kitty was at Bellingham's airport when two missionary pilots from California arrived requesting fuel. Their two rear seats were empty and auxiliary tanks were crammed into the baggage area behind those seats. Kitty was intrigued. They said they were bound for Ethiopia to help with Moody Bible Institute missionary projects and that they planned to depart at five the next morning. Kitty called and discussed the details with Kimball.

He said, "Let's go with them!"

Kitty and Kimball talked with Kimball's father, Judge Marshall Forrest, about climbing into the rear seats for the flight to Africa.

"You kids know there's a civil war brewing there, don't you?" he asked emphatically.

The Ethiopian Civil War Forrest was referring to began in 1974 after the ousting of the Ethiopian Emperor, Haile Selassie. News of the junta had made international newspaper headlines. But it didn't stop Kitty or Kimball. They took sleeping bags and slept overnight in the airport office to be on site when the men arrived in the early morning, only to be disappointed. One of the men told them that not only did they need to have more flight experience, they also needed to be members of their sponsoring Christian Institute. Undeterred, Kitty and Kimball ran after them as they fired up and were taxing out to depart.

"How about if we just come along for the ride?" they called out over the sound of the engines. The men shook their heads. "It would be too cramped," they said. Little did they know they had two 75-gallon gas tanks in the back.

They continued their taxi to the active runway and Kitty and Kimball watched as they took to the skies. Kitty knew somehow there would be other openings, other chances that would come her way. She noted in her diary a quote from Peterson, "The art of work is doing your present work so well that it will open doors to new opportunities. Tasks done at a high standard pave the way to bigger things."

Those words rang true with her job as "Little Gas Gal" when she joined the Ninety-Nines, an international organization of women pilots, and participated in her chapter as a reporter for their newsletter. Her first journalism assignment was the Abbotsford International Air Show of 1974, an exciting event staged annually in British Columbia. With her official press pass, Kitty mingled with the performers. She witnessed her ground school instructor, Joann Osterud, do her first air show performance flying clipped-wing Cub aerobatics. Kitty also watched the Canadian Forces Skyhawks parachute team and a demonstration of a search-and-rescue by a team flying a CC-115 Buffalo. The most extraordinary moment of the event was when she was introduced to King Hussein of Jordan, the special invited guest and host of the show. She was also extended an invitation to fly in formation in one of the beautiful Canadair CT-114 Tutor jets piloted by the Canadian Forces demonstration team, the Snowbirds.

Joanne Osterud,
Kitty's ground school instructor

Reporting on the performances for the Ninety-Nines, Kitty had prominent front row access to the famed air show and had an incredible opportunity to talk with the Squadron Commander and pilots of the Snowbirds. She was invited along with other media members and air show performers to climb into the right seat of one of the sleek, low-winged, aerobatic jet trainers for her special introduction to high performance multi-aircraft precision aerobatics-and a participation in aviation history. After an hour of briefing, Kitty donned a loaned fireproof suit and a helmet and climbed aboard. Six jets, all equipped with side-by-side seats and bubble canopies, took off in formation, and as soon as they were airborne, climbed into a loop. Wingtips overlapped by a mere four feet.

While flying maneuvers in a diamond slot formation around the Northern Cascades she heard over the radio, "Smoke on, Snowbirds!"

The team did a controlled split, and when they were a safe distance from the others, the pilot announced, "It's your plane."

Kitty took the controls briefly to perform a roll and was surprised when the jet rolled 365 degrees not just once, but two times before she could neutralize the control stick. Glancing to her left after relinquishing

Snowbirds performance,
Abbotsford International Air Show, BC
Kitty got a ride & turn at
the controls, 1974

the controls, Kitty marveled at the smoothness of the routine. Sliding from one formation to another seemed effortless, as if the pilot barely moved his feet or the stick. As they rolled into a bank, the sucking pull of positive G's effectively doubled her weight, pulling her body into the seat and making her hands too heavy to lift. Rolling into a tight spin, the ground rotated around the craft's nose much faster than she'd ever experienced with the Bücker. During the 7G pullout followed by a -3G's in the loop, she tightened her muscles in her thighs, stomach and forearms. Kitty's mind went grey, and then for a matter of seconds, black. She regained her vision as the team was landing. It was a thrilling, unforgettable ride.

Making his first appearance at that air show was King Hussein bin Talal of Jordan, a pilot and prominent aviation enthusiast. He saw Dave Rahm perform his impressive low-level performance in his Bücker Jungmann and subsequently invited Rahm and fellow air show star, Steve Wolf, to travel to Jordan to initiate an aerobatic demonstration team called the Royal Jordanian Falcons. Their talents would become monumental to the Jordanians. Formed two years later by Rahm and Wolf, the Royal Jordanian Falcons racked up a long history of successes.

Kitty & Dave Rham in the Bücker Jungmann

Unfortunately, Dave Rahm didn't live to see them. An accident in Amman in 1976 was fatal. He was performing a lomcevak combined with a tail slide and hammerhead when he hit the ground. King Hussein was seen running to Rahm's burning airplane to pull him out, but the impact had killed him. Dave Rahm's passing was a profound loss. Kitty remembered flying with him in the biplane from the northwest all the way to Hales Corner, Wisconsin, the first home of the Experimental Aircraft Association. It was as if they had flown backward in time, back to aviation's Golden Era with open cockpit, helmets, goggles and even the rudimentary communication system that worked for them as it had for air pioneers. They wore parachutes and for warmth at altitude, Kitty cocooned herself into a puffy down jacket.

When Rahm had something to say or to ask, he passed notes forward to Kitty. "Do you want to do a snap roll, hammerhead stall, or outside loop?"

She would often gesture a 'thumb up' or a 'thumb down.' They flew over the Grand Tetons and the Bitterroots, rolling around points, climbing up and over into perfect loops, flying on knife-edge and streaking through the air as if they were the first to fly over the age-old mountains. They left no imprints other than the swirling clouds roiled into vortices by the wake of their passing. When they touched down on the close-cut grass strip in Wisconsin, Kitty's father and brother, Denny, were waiting for them in Denny's Cessna 310. With the right engine shut down, Kitty climbed into the modern twin-engine Cessna, and it felt as if she was climbing from the past to the future of aviation.

Montana has a long string of airway beacons for night Mt. flying.

Good chance to see a lot of mule deer through here, Antelope later on toward + beyond Bozeman.

Smoke is on—

Lewis + Clark + Sacajawea came down this river. (W. [dermess])

are Bitterroots—

behind a Mt. your right shoulder

High Mts over

We will soon fly over the WWSC Fall geology camp— they are down there now— I'll rock the wing when I think they might see us.

World's biggest smokestack is at end of valley coming up on right. Anaconda copper smelter — makes smog.

Once in awhile I check mags + you notice a short change in engine sound—

Just crossed cont. divide— all rivers flow to Atlantic now—

Town is Boulder, Mont.

Helena way off to left—

Came through that pass in big snowstorm in Ca tabria

I used to do geology through all these valleys. Have you noticed the faded limestones?

Dave Rahm flight notes from the Bücker Jungmann flight

Carolyn Cullen, Val, & Kitty, Oak Bluff Airport, Martha's Vineyard

CHAPTER FIVE

Being Yourself

John Banner, Mary Murphy, Brent Coleman at Sandy Cove on Bellingham Bay, Washington

"By the grace of God, you are what you are; glory in your selfhood, accept yourself, and go on from there..."

—Peterson

Life-altering change was ushered in during the autumn of Kitty's senior year at Bellingham. Kitty lived on Lake Samish in Bellingham's Chuckanut Range of the Cascade Mountains, a series of highly varied hills and valleys unique to the entire Pacific Northwest. From the commanding and rugged Mt. Baker, Mt. Shuksan and the alpine country, the Chuckanuts descend into rolling and forested foothills. The sole such occurrence in the Cascades, this range extends westerly enough to reach salt water. Between the Skagit and Nooksack river systems, the resulting corridor connects the mountains with the waters of Puget Sound and forms a treasured region of meadows, lakes, streams and wetlands.

Brent Coleman, a pre-med student, was a friend of Kitty. Coleman lived in a magical little cottage in Sandy Cove on Bellingham Bay, Washington State. His father was a vice president with Exxon and his family had moved often when he was younger, living in Australia and Japan. Coleman had an avid love for crab fishing and he would occasionally cook crab for Kitty at his cottage and make his three-layer corn bread.

One morning, Coleman decided to go crabbing and Kitty agreed to meet him after her flight. To contribute to the dinner, Kitty volunteered to dig for clams. She borrowed mud boots, a shovel and a bucket from a neighbor and drove her pickup to Sandy Cove. Having spent more time at the airport than she intended, she arrived late, so she parked in Coleman's driveway and took a shortcut by walking across the estuary. If it had been the cool of early morning, things would have gone quite differently. But it was afternoon and tidal conditions were different. As Kitty walked along toting the shovel and pail with the borrowed boots over her jeans, she suddenly felt her lower legs sucked downward. She attempted to pull out her legs from the spot, but every time she moved her feet her legs were sucked down again. She was only about 100 feet from shore, but panic set in. Every move made things worse. She felt powerless to stop it.

Kitty looked around frantically. She was totally alone; there was nobody to see or hear her and she was sinking. She tried lifting a knee to get one leg out and then tried to raise the other leg. The more she struggled, the deeper she went. She looked up whenever she heard an airplane and swung her arms over her head, hoping the pilots would see that she was in trouble and radio for help. But the yelling, waving and struggling only seemed to speed the process and the deeper she sunk. She clawed at the surface mud, trying for traction. Nothing worked. Then, to her horror, she saw that the tide was coming in. By that point, the sludge was all the way up over her thighs and her clothes were being pulled from her body.

The borrowed boots and her socks were first to go. She could feel them being scraped off her feet and legs. Her jeans, heavy with slime, were next. They disappeared with a sound she could actually hear-a slow, terrifying slurp. Kitty realized that if the muck got a good grip on her sweatshirt, escape would be impossible. She would be swallowed alive and no one knew where she was.

She raised her arms, pulling her sweatshirt up and over her head and out of the gross mass. Even that effort caused her to sink lower. She reasoned she would never escape if she didn't stop fighting the vile sand that was home to so many creatures but alien to her. She was fighting a losing battle. In desperation, Kitty used both hands to flatten the shovel on the surface. She pushed her chest against it. The shovel gave her leverage. Slowly, she began to sidle like a crab toward the shore. In what seemed like forever, Kitty finally clawed at what felt like the first solid ground. She was exhausted. Her clothes, borrowed boots and bucket had all disappeared. She collapsed, covered completely in the foul-smelling low tide mud.

Naked and covered with dank mud, she lay there long enough to catch her breath. The weight of the mud on her body was incredible. When she finally summoned enough energy to stand, she wandered back through the woods, headed for her Datsun pickup in Coleman's driveway. It was then she heard tree limbs cracking behind her. With adrenaline already flowing through her, Kitty began running through the trees. Finally, she turned around to confront whatever was following her and could scarcely believe her eyes. Close on her heels was a long-horned goat. She turned and ran. Much later, she could laugh at the irony, that of all things to be pursued by, it was a goat. But at the time, she couldn't reach the safety of her pickup fast enough.

Later, Kitty returned the shovel to her neighbor, offering to pay for his lost boots and bucket. He was aghast when she described her close call.

He said, "Don't you know animals get trapped in the mud flats all the time and perish? You could have died!"

She thought of the fossilized bones in La Brea Tar Pits and the uncanny images of animals' wills to live. She thought, "When you struggle and give in to panic, you lose all capability of rational thought." Stuck in the mud, Kitty had nearly lost it.

After telling Rahm of her nearly fatal brush with the mud flat, he based an entire lecture on her experience to educate his geology students on pore water pressure. Rahm explained the science behind the quick-mud: seawater introduced into sediment during high tide creates a thick, congealing mass as the tide recedes and returns. She would be often reminded of her experience and the science of it as Rahm explained it when she later worked at the Houston Oil and Minerals based in Anchorage, Alaska.

In the fall of 1974, the newly graduated 22-year-old Kitty returned to the Midwest to spend time at her family's beloved cottage in Three Lakes, Wisconsin. The fall weather was mild that year and colorful trees encircled Medicine Lake with rich golden, orange and red foliage. When the wind was still, the trees doubled their own beauty in mirrored reflections that rippled on the water's surface. When down by the pier, a mild breeze brought the familiar pungent odors of fish and the smoke from wood fires and piles of burning leaves.

A good friend of hers, Mary Beth Griffin, was in town for her wedding. At the Banner cottage, the popular sport that summer consisted of parachuting on a towline behind Kitty's brother Jim's jet boat. They had devised a method of takeoff similar to assisting a glider's wingtips during launch by those running alongside. Instead of having the parachutist skim his or her body through the water while the boat accelerated and the chute filled with air, a couple of people on the hill in front of the cottage would hold the parachute open so it was ready for lift off. The boat would idle to pull the line taut, then the driver would hit the throttle as the parachutist, upright and harnessed, would run a few leaping steps downhill toward the water. After only two or three running steps, the chute would become airborne, lifting like a bird catching an invisible updraft.

Kitty's brother, John, was driving the jet boat and the pick-up boat was docked at the end of the pier ready to follow. Kitty invited Mary Beth to take a turn, but she declined. She had never tried the sport, and with her wedding so close, she was hesitant. Kitty thought she'd make one soaring pass and then, seeing how it was done, Mary Beth might want a turn. Kitty slipped into a wet suit and fastened the harness securely. No one noticed the riser lines to the chute were twisted. The moment she was airborne, a short crosswind blast aggravated the twisted lines. With the boat speeding up, the chute spun into a roll and headed straight for the pick-up boat. Kitty tucked and turned, but couldn't avoid the inevitable. She crashed hard, thigh first, into the fiberglass bow, through the windshield, and down into the boat, back first into the gunwale. She was then yanked up out of the boat, skipping several times on the water to a stop.

At first, Kitty couldn't move her legs. She strained to unhook the risers, struggled out of the harness, and stumbled all the way up the hill and into the cottage, her body in shock. She wanted desperately to get into the shower, to get heat on her back, to wash away some of the blood. The pain was intense and it became more agonizing by the moment. Her brother drove her to the clinic in the nearby town in the pickup truck where the doctor simply scolded her for what had happened. They left, and in attempt to cheer Kitty up, John took her to the local airport to watch planes in the pattern doing takeoffs and landings before heading home.

Mary Beth insisted they go to the Rhinelander Hospital. The diagnosis was a lumbar spine compression fracture. Her third vertebra had been crushed against her fourth and gouged out part of the fifth. More than just crushed bone, she'd damaged muscles, nerves and ligaments.

Kitty spent several weeks in the hospital where a kind Indian lady knitted her a very long scarf that stretched from her bed, out the door and down the hall. On the third day, she regained feeling in her legs. When she was finally released, she left the hospital in a custom full back brace. She spent one more night at the cottage before her dad and a close friend with a station wagon cautiously loaded her onto a mattress to be transferred to her parents' home in Chicago for a seemingly endless stay.

Kitty's aunt Marge was visiting at the cottage with her friends, whose son was a member of the USAF Aerial Demonstration Squadron as a Thunderbird pilot. Prior to leaving Bellingham, Kitty had seen the Thunderbirds perform in Everett, Washington. At that air show, she had a small pamphlet signed by one of the pilots to whom she was introduced. Kitty's dad helped her pull out the pamphlet during her aunt's visit. The sole signature was that of her friends' son. Later, Kitty would receive a large photo signed by all of the Thunderbird team members with 'Best Wishes' and 'Good Luck' messages for Kitty's recovery.

Confined to her bedroom in her parents' home in Chicago, Kitty hung the photo on her bedroom wall. She needed all the encouragement possible. It would be close to a year before she was well. Desperate to heal, Kitty kept herself busy by reading books. The book *Alive*, which told the story of the soccer players who survived a plane crash in the Andes Mountains, particularly moved her. Reading stories of other peoples' strengths in the face of adversity inspired her and raised her spirits.

Although confined with a back brace, Kitty was ambulatory by May, 1975. She had endured the recuperation but her restlessness was growing. She was eager to close her aviation books and leave the confines of her bedroom.

Kitty decided to visit Stephanie Forrest in Annapolis, Maryland. She headed east in her Datsun pickup, and with navigation confirmed from several toll booth attendants, arrived at Stephanie's in the middle of the night. The next morning, the two sailed out into the bay in a Dragon sailboat. The day after that, they drove to Assateague Island to spend two nights camping in the sand dunes.

Stephanie had been studying astronomy, and while they lay in the soft, warm sand, basking under the canopy of millions of stars, Stephanie plotted them. The heavens were brilliant, unhampered by city lights. Kitty listened intently as Stephanie named off particular stars and planets, grateful to be a part of the open skies once again. She told Stephanie of her plans to return west and take courses at Colorado Aero Tech in Broomfield, Colorado. She believed the technical school specialized in exactly the areas that she was lacking. While her brothers had learned a great deal about maintenance while working on their own vehicles and at the family's heating and construction business, she never spent a lot of time tinkering with cars or learning about mechanics. She wanted to earn her mechanics license. She wanted to understand more about what was going on under the cowl of an aircraft. The heartbeat of an airplane was its engine.

"And," she added, "I want to go to Alaska."

While Kitty's mother, Helen, encouraged her children to choose their own directions and create their own destinies, she would not necessarily have chosen Alaskan pilot and mechanic for her daughter. That Christmas, while Kitty's cousin, Susie Stanton, who was attending Johnson and Wales to become a chef, was asking for a Masterchef knife set for Christmas, Kitty asked to receive a stocked "Master" toolbox. It was a Christmas wish that went unanswered, yet Kitty would receive an even more beneficial gift.

Her parents had befriended a childless couple. The McClains, were repeatedly invited to share important celebrations like Thanksgiving and Christmas with the Banners. Mr. McClain showed his gratitude by seeing that upon his death, Kitty and each of her siblings received $8,000. This generous inheritance saw Kitty through her pilot certificate, some of her college expenses and a start in maintenance training at Colorado Aero Tech. She was the only woman among 300 men, all who were on the G.I. Bill and Man Power Grants.

Kitty felt obligated to pay the rest of her expenses on her own while avoiding being saddled with loans with no means of repayment.

Still recovering and in a back brace, she was limited in her activities and couldn't think about a strenuous job. Low on money, she left Aero Tech after a few months and took a job at the Boulder Airport, fueling airplanes once again.

During that time, Kitty met John Wolff and received an intriguing invitation to travel. Wolff, an architectural graduate student, was a New Yorker studying at the University of Colorado in Boulder. He invited her to spend time with his family over the Christmas holiday. They would visit Riverdale, New York, as well as his parents' second home in

Edgartown on Martha's Vineyard, Massachusetts, where John was collaborating with architect Tom Lyons to renovate Wolff's 1800's Martha's Vineyard home. That year, there would also be a magnificent sailing of the Tall Ships as heralded celebrations of the country's 1976 Bicentennial.

While reading Nancy Harkness Love's biography about the Women's Auxiliary Ferrying Squadron (WAFS) during World War II, Kitty discovered that one member of the WAFS and WASP, the Women Air Force Service Pilots, lived on Martha's Vineyard. Carolyn Cullen was owner-operator of the private strip at Oak Bluffs, Trade Winds Airport.

Carolyn Cullen, Oak Bluff Airport, Martha's Vineyard

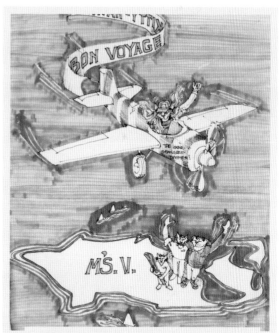

Martha's Vineyard by Tom Lyon

Kitty heard Cullen's name mentioned as she traveled with John on the ferry from Martha's Vineyard and was eager to meet her. But Christmas vacation was over and she needed to return to Colorado and look for employment that could keep body and soul together as she continued her studies.

Seeking a job at Boulder's Municipal Airport seemed logical. Kitty was accepted for a position to greet aerial arrivals, refuel their aircraft and welcome transient and resident pilots. She took advantage of The Cloud Base glider school, home to the Flatirons, which was based out of the Boulder Airport and received a glider certificate in a SGS 233 Schweitzer.

In the 1970s, the majority of private pilots were male. Kitty's arrival on the scene at Boulder's airport did not go unnoticed. With her enthusiasm, Kitty attracted interest from the aviation community. She wasn't in the job for long before a friend, John Ruger, a U.S. Team cross-country skier, introduced her to Jim Sharp, a Boulder resident and an accomplished pilot. Jim wasted no time inviting her for a sightseeing ride above Boulder. He rolled out his Cessna 180 single-engine, tail-wheel-equipped aircraft and the two climbed aboard.

Kitty jumped in the right seat and during their initial takeoff roll, Sharp shut the engine down and told her to get out with the fire extinguisher. Apparently, he'd been having engine issues. After a quick inspection, they got back into the Cessna, fired up and took off for a flight around the Boulder Flatirons.

The engine caused no fires, but between the two pilots, a mutual respect had been sparked. Later, Sharp was heard to have said, "A guy has to have a few tricks up his sleeve with a lady like Kitty."

Sharp's talent with flying the aircraft was compelling. Jim had personally known and had flown with Don. Kitty was also impressed with his work with German filmmaker, Martin Schliessler, in Alaska. Sharp had worked to edit film in Schliessler's studio in Baden-Baden, Germany, and traveled to Nepal to assist him on a shoot. His ploy left a permanent memory in her mind and they developed a close friendship.

On the flyleaf of James Greiner's 1974 biography, *Wager With The Wind, The Don Sheldon Story*, is the telling description of this remarkable adventurer and extraordinarily talented pilot, famous for his exploits in the Alaskan Bush and on Alaskan Glaciers: "Perhaps nowhere else on earth is there still a breed of daring, rugged individualists to match the bush pilots of Alaska. And Don Sheldon, one of the few pilots who made high-risk mountain flying a full-time job, is a legend among this special group."

Sheldon succumbed to cancer in January 1975. Sharp, who spent time with Sheldon, bought Talkeetna Air Taxi from Sheldon's widow, Roberta. He, in turn, invited Kitty to come with him to Alaska. To have him even broach the subject of Alaska was amazing enough, but he asked her to come work for him in Talkeetna during the summer of 1976. A job in Alaska! It came so suddenly and was so wonderfully tempting, it was as if her whole life to that point was coalescing at the exact place she was meant to be. Alaska. Kitty was aware of the importance of taking time to consider the entire situation, and although it was difficult to refuse, she weighed prior plans against this amazing invitation. She finally had to admit that although she would love to travel to Alaska, the timing was off and such a move was premature. Her back, though much improved, was not fully recovered and was not yet as resilient and strong as a long-distance move and the physical requirements of a flying job would require. Packing and lifting alone required heavy work she was not yet able to perform; her recovery would span another year.

She had made a commitment to her friend, the architect John Wolff, to help with his restoration project of their Victorian house. She had already requested time off from the Boulder Airport to work with John and with Tom Lyons on Martha's Vineyard as an expediter on the project. Additionally, she introduced herself to Carolyn Cullen, writing her to see if there was work at the airport that summer. The answer was, "yes".

Kitty's Datsun truck was destined to come in very handy for pickup and delivery of a variety of building materials. The trip to Massachusetts and the island proved to be a multiple blessing. Carolyn Cullen would be a great help to her budding aviation career and another great chance to work with and learn from a pro.

When she arrived on the island, Kitty placed a call to Carolyn Cullen and set up a time for a meeting. Kitty walked into her Trade Winds office and came face-to-face with a small but strong blonde, pony-tailed woman with the most amazingly intense eyes. As they heartily shook hands, the surrounding memorabilia of Cullen's flying life that decorated and made unique her small office mesmerized Kitty. Ocean flying was intriguing. Part of the allure came in fueling the spotters for swordfish fishermen. Equipped with auxiliary fuel tanks, they flew out over the Atlantic and reported their finds to respective fishing boats. It wasn't as easy as it sounds. They spent a long time over water, a good venue for floatplanes but not land planes. During Kitty's work that summer, one of the spotters never returned.

Carolyn Cullen knew Amelia Earhart. One of Earhart's flying jackets was left at the small airport after she came by to see Carolyn before her transatlantic flight. Working with Cullen was a pleasure, yet she was also a very private person. Kitty respected her privacy and unabashedly admired that she'd been a WASP, had graduated in Class 44-W-6, and flew the training aircraft common to the experience of most of the women pilots: PT-17, BT-13, and the UC-78. She knew that there was much she could learn from this accomplished and experienced woman pilot.

Carolyn had been stationed at Marfa and Gardner Army air bases, and although she was no longer a young woman, she still flew with the authority she derived from her military training. She was a taskmaster, and when Kitty flew with her, she tolerated no nonsense. One of her first orders to Kitty was to take off her shoes and fly in bare feet to be more sensitive and more responsive to vibrations of the rudder pedals. She expected Kitty to be on altitude, airspeed and attitude without any equivocation and she was as tidy with her aerial demands as she was with her equipment.

Her hangar was immaculate and her tools carefully stored. She lived in her Quonset hut right off the airport, but she rarely invited anybody there. Cullen described having adopted several burros from the Grand Canyon to save them from being slaughtered. Kitty greatly admired her conviction.

Kitty by Tom Lyon

One day in Massachusetts, Kitty told Cullen about the offer from Talkeetna with the Air Taxi and she predicted, "You'll be in Alaska before the summer comes to an end."

That summer of 1976, a serious hurricane threatened the island. Kitty was an extra pair of hands for Cullen. With her back stronger, together they bolted down the hangars, wedged everything with wood and secured all loose items that might have been picked up or destroyed by high winds and waves. She came to greatly appreciate Kitty's help.

Shortly after the hurricane, Kitty received an envelope from Jim Sharp. The letter included a Polaroid of himself and his airplane on a glacier in Alaska. Her desire to go to Alaska was renewed. She finally had to admit to Cullen that she was right. The summer wasn't quite over, but Kitty's back was healthy and strong again. In August, Kitty made up her mind. She was going to travel to Alaska.

In a rare departure from her normal reticence to invite anyone to her personal living quarters, Carolyn Cullen extended an invitation to Kitty, who recalled, "In the months I worked there, I'd not been invited to her Quonset hut. Then, she and her partner, Val Colebrook, invited me to dinner. I was more than amazed. The hut was a veritable museum with a host of paraphernalia from the 1940s and World War II."

As Kitty went to leave, Cullen extended her hand. She was clasping a wad of bills, which she pressed into Kitty's hand.

Kitty said, "Oh, no. I can't take this."

She quipped back, "Take it. I know you're going to need it."

She was right about that, too. Kitty needed every penny. As she drove west to spend time with her parents, her trusty Datsun finally broke down. She had taken back roads, thinking it would be great to see more of the country and not be gazing solely at interstate highways. It was her alternator that went out in the middle of nowhere. Kitty had to arrange for her car to be towed and found that the alternator needed to be replaced. She used every bit of the money Cullen gave her.

A month later Kitty wrote to her, "I'm in Alaska. I came for the flying job I had turned down earlier. I have much to learn about flying Alaska, but I think I will keep my shoes on!'"

Fairview Bar, Talkeetna Alaska

CHAPTER SIX

Awareness

Talkeetna welcome sign

"Awareness is searching for beauty everywhere, in a flower, a mountain, a machine..."

—Peterson

On his way to Alaska, Jim Sharp and his friend, John Ruger, flew into a vicious storm in southern Idaho. As night fell, Sharp's Cessna 180 started to ice up. They lost some instruments and Sharp chose to head down to a lower altitude. During their descent, the ice-coated windshield exploded into the cabin, its shards breaking Sharp's nose. His glasses and sundry loose items whipped out into the blustery night.

A wall of wind blowing at 150 mph suddenly poured into their faces. Sharp glanced at Ruger and saw to his horror that Ruger's "Hair was peeled back from his scalp." He struggled to control the ice-coated aircraft with the airflow over the tail disturbed and the airplane buffeting violently. Sharp turned on the landing lights into the blur of driven snow and identified a couple of hills ahead. They were going in. He lowered the flaps, reduced the power and landed, rolling a short way before hitting a snowdrift and flipping tail over nose.

The two men crawled out through the space created by the smashed windshield and stood together in the blowing snow to shake one another's hands, knowing they were both lucky to be alive. A nearby rancher who arrived at the scene confirmed their good fortune, telling them, "Yeah, boys, I've had four crashes on my place here, sits right under the airway... You boys are the lucky ones. Yes sir, you're the only ones that survived."

Surface memories of accidents can be pushed to the darkest corners of memory, but lingering doubts are impossible to eradicate. After his survival, Sharp would never be able to completely erase the trauma from the accident. Yet he now owned Sheldon's Air Taxi business as well as the Cessna that replaced the 180 lost in Idaho. He had a new set of parameters for his life.

For her part, Kitty was aware that her choice to become part of the bush piloting scene would lead to rare experiences, but ones that were also fraught with challenges and risks. In Alaska, it was imperative that pilots had intimate understandings of the topography, weather patterns and weather conditions of the region, a knowledge that could only be attained through doing. Over time, Kitty would be crossing an unknown, unforgiving wilderness, facing turbulence and unpredictable weather patterns for which mountains are famous, reacting to surprises such as sudden gusts of wild swirling winds, and having to make quick decisions when faced with storms, icing, low-level fog, or spongy wetlands of the

First Talkeetna Air Taxi (TAT)
Office & Sheldon Cub

tundra. She was acutely aware that, as pilot-in-command, she might have to make emergency landings, and would be assuming responsibility for her passengers amidst a rugged terrain and among animals that required anticipation, knowledge and a healthy respect. Her sense of adventure stiffened her resolve. Rather than giving in to any fright, Kitty became even more determined to succeed.

In 1976, the village of Talkeetna, Alaska, had a population of a few hundred people, and almost as many stray dogs. The locals are a colorful breed. Some say it is the freedom Alaska's last frontier offers. Others say it's the friendly spirit of anything goes. Certainly, they all must be able to handle the feeling that a 40-mph wind gives you at 30 below zero.

Located where three massive rivers join roaring down from Mt. McKinley, it was originally an Athabascan native village discovered by white men searching for gold in the early 1900s. Talkeetna quickly transformed into a booming mining and trapping town, complete with general store and an equal number of bars and churches. Unfortunately, white men brought

Talkeetna Airport (TKA) & Village Air Strip aerial view

tuberculosis, wiping out the entire native Indian population. Daylight lasts nearly 24 hours in the summertime and temperatures hover in the mid-sixties and low seventies. Winters are long, cold and dark. When spring arrives, the pace picks up in town as the local people earn a living with the tourists and climbers before the snow and cold return.

Talkeetna is the launching point for mountaineers attempting to climb Denali - Athabaskan for "The Great One" - North America's tallest mountain at 20,310 feet (formerly Mt. McKinley). Climbers are transported via aircraft up to the Kahiltna base camp at 7,200 feet and trek on their own from there. Annually, more than 1,200 mountaineers arrive from some 40 countries from May through July. Roughly 52 percent reach the summit and a small percentage die each year. Pilots provide transportation and are a lifeline for climbers, both in air search or rescues in an emergency.

Working with Carolyn Cullen on Martha's Vineyard helped Kitty build her confidence and skills in the cockpit, but nothing truly prepared Kitty for the challenging, dramatic, and unpredictable experiences of Alaska bush flying. She had heard of Talkeetna's reputation among outdoorsmen as the jumping-off point for climbers, skiers, fishermen, kayakers, hunters and the adventurous. She also

knew that Alaska was a haven for pilots because of its limited roads and vast distances to traverse.

Denali from Susitna River, Talkeetna

Kitty spoke with her brother, John, suggesting the two fly to Alaska in his Cessna 182, but a leak in one of his airplane's extended fuel bladders meant commercial airlines for Kitty. Still, landing in Anchorage filled her with adrenaline.

The commercial terminal is a veritable museum, displaying preserved Alaskan flora and fauna. The corridors sport huge trophy game like polar and grizzly bears, some rearing on their back legs with the claws of their front paws extended menacingly as if to grasp a spawning Coho or Sockeye. Kitty slowed down to take it all in. She re-imagined herself a pilot who would be flying over unknown lands that belonged to hordes of indigenous animals and plant life. Close to the bears are exhibits of fine handmade native crafts in glass cases. Under her breath, she attempted pronouncing their tribal names, "Inupiat, Aleut, Tlingit, Haida." She took notice of the tribes closest to Talkeetna - the Athabascan Ingalik and Tanaina - known for their supple smoked moose hide and woven porcupine quillwork.

Jim Sharp met Kitty in the baggage area and took her over to his Cessna 180 floatplane, which was waiting at the Lake Hood Seaplane Base. Sharp explained that the airplane was once property of the legendary bush pilot, Don Sheldon. To be sitting in Sheldon's aircraft felt unreal. At the water's edge, the two climbed aboard the seaplane and fastened their seatbelts and shoulder harnesses. Sharp started the engine, contacted air traffic control, and *74 X-Ray* was sequenced among a queue of taxiing aircraft jockeying for takeoff positions. They snaked their way past a vast and colorful array of amphibious aircraft, most moored and waiting for owners and tourists to explore Alaska's versatile mode of flying. Even though she'd heard of Lake Hood's reputation as the busiest and largest floatplane base in the world, the fall season brought an especially feverish flying activity and a parade of extraordinary aircraft. As Sharp added power, she glanced around to watch water spray from their floats. The floats broke clear of the friction

Jim Sharp on Kahiltna Glacier

Jim Sharp in Cub

holding them to the water and the airplane climbed away on a northbound heading. She admired the city of Anchorage as they cruised above it before letting her eyes roam along the roughly serrated mountain range ahead that was drawing them northward.

The next morning, she noted in her diary, "October 1, 1976: ALASKA!" She added, "Spent night at Stephan Lake Lodge, eating sourdough pancakes made by Don Lee over a custom built 55-gallon drum stove in the cabin. The crisp exterior of the giant pancake was so inviting, but as I cut in for my first bite, the liquid batter came pouring out." With her usual good humor, she decorated the diary entry with a bold star and added that she'd told Lee, "They're great! Would love your recipe!"

A day later the entry was, "Flew with Jim around McKinley and Alaskan range in C185 with Canadians. Stopped in at an old gold mine and had coffee with the guys. Snow began to fall."

A couple days later, Ray Genet, famous mountaineer on Denali, sought Kitty's help. It involved Martin Schliessler, who in addition to making a film, was a floatplane pilot and part-owner of Stephan Lake Lodge. The lodge was a magnificent A-frame that catered to limited groups of hunters and fishermen who enjoyed upscale surroundings, excellent food and prized results from returning victorious from the hunt for sheep or moose or having fished for Rainbow Trout, Arctic Grayling, or King, Sockeye and Coho Salmon.

*Stephan Lake,
securing the external load*

Genet contacted Sharp and Kitty with the news that Martin Schliessler had run into trouble on Murder Lake. He was caught by a surprisingly common and dangerous downdraft known to exist during approach or departure from a lake. The strong eddy pulled Schliessler's floatplane out of the air and slammed him onto the shore upside down. Genet and Sharp had flown the Cessna 180 floatplane from Talkeetna to offer assistance after Martin freed himself from the craft. They helped remove his aircraft floats, and one at a time, ferried them back to Stephan Lake, by tying them on the outside of Sharp's Cessna 180.

Kitty noted in her diary, "On the second run from Talkeetna, Jim and I loaded and flew three plywood sheets straddled across the top of the floats to the lodge and we flew out the second damaged float. A first-time exterior load experience for me."

Ray Genet "The Pirate"

Floatplane Rescue at Murder Lake

Days later, Genet, Sharp, and Kitty hoisted the floats onto the truck in Talkeetna for Kitty to deliver to the Wasilla area for repair. Genet roped the two floats down. Kitty later discovered, to her surprise, that he had not cross-roped the load. As she drove down the highway toward Wasilla, a strong gust of wind split the floats apart. Still somewhat attached, the tips came down on either side of the truck, pinning the windows and doors shut and allowing the floats to scrape on the asphalt. Kitty didn't slam on the brakes, yet even with gentle brake pressure, she couldn't get stopped without unleashing a shower of sparks from the base of the floats that spun up toward the truck. With the exposed fuel tank, she realized she was sitting in a potential bomb. While she couldn't see any leak, she could smell gas fumes, and she realized she was trapped.

Luckily, a stranger drove by, took one look, and pulled to a stop to help. He quickly untied the floats so she could hop out of the truck. They readjusted the floats on the truck, cross-tied them together and she was on her way with a valuable lesson learned: always check that load yourself!

For a break, Sharp treated Kitty to a fishing trip in the crystal-clear waters of Clarence Lake. She reported, "We landed-*74* at the lake in light rain misting into the silent water. Soon, I was perched on one of the aircraft floats casting toward shadows I'd seen swimming close to the surface. Within seconds, the biggest Arctic Grayling I'd ever seen was dancing on the line. I reeled it in, unhooked, and following Jim's lead, quickly slid the fish into the water in the floatplane floats via the inspection plate cover."

While they fished, the water seeped in through leaky rivets in the floats, creating a perfect environment to keep fish fresh. Today the stashing of fish in floatplane floats is no longer legal in Alaska because hungry bears caught on and began destroying floatplane floats to get to the catch.

Boyd Haines

"That's kind of a rule in Alaska, no fish in the floats," chuckled Lee, now a designated pilot examiner in Talkeetna.

Early on, Kitty was pilot for the "milk run," a regular delivery of mail and groceries to people out in the bush. One of her most interesting customers was Boyd Haines, an elderly man cloistered up at Rainy Pass. Old Man Haines was a rangy, toothless trapper with a mysterious history. He always looked forward to the hum of the engine that would arrive with his toiletries, beer and social security checks. Kitty delighted in surprising him with delicacies like fresh ice cream and strawberries; items he hadn't ordered and probably hadn't seen in years. He invariably invited her into his digs, pouring cup after unwashed cup of coffee for her.

Boyd Haines gathers martens to create a fur collar for Kitty.

Boyd Haines' digs

Boyd Haines receives his propane delivery from Kitty

He hadn't always been their customer. He was discovered by mistake one spring day on a rare backhaul from the other side of the Alaska Range frantically waving a red towel on a stick, according to Sharp. After a long, cold winter, he'd run out of firewood. He burned his outhouse and ramshackle outbuildings for heat and by that point was desperate for a ride out to get supplies.

Kitty told Kate Sheldon, "The turbulence through the pass to get to Haines was bordering on severe. I had to really strap down to keep my head from slamming into the top of the cockpit!"

When his supplies turned up that first time, Old Man Haines came out dragging a canoe over the ice-rimmed shoreline, shouting, "Hallelujah." He was visibly relieved that they had returned.

"Haines was in his 80s, didn't have a lot of teeth and you couldn't always make out what he was saying," recalled Kitty.

He shoved the canoe to Kitty. They piled the supplies and tied the fuel barrels to it before she pushed the canoe back to him. Old Man Haines was quite a character, especially the part about a hole on his property with a sign proclaiming, 'Miranda's Resting Place-she fell in and never got out.' Kitty could never figure out if he had named his outhouse or if he had a pet animal that had fallen in. "Coulda' been based on something mythological," Lee guessed. "Or something from a poem. Haines was fairly well read despite the way he lived."

His main residence was an old Army tent covered like chain mail with aluminum newspaper print plates. They were the size of a double newspaper page and frequently listed for sale in the Anchorage newspaper.

Mike Fisher with homebuilt

"You could still read the printing on them," Mike Fisher explained. "We'd get a couple hundred of them into an airplane. They're real lightweight and only cost 25 cents apiece." But surprisingly, Haines made a good roof out of them. "Ol' Boyd Haines poked a hole in 'em with an ice pick and fastened them to his tent with wire. It was his new roof and siding. Miles away on a clear day it would stand out, a gleaming fixture in the distance," Fisher said. "Seems like kind of a dumb idea, but it worked for him. He needed to keep the wind out. He always said that house was the only place he was happy," Fisher said.

Haines had names for all the wild animals in his area and was always eager to regale Kitty with the latest of his questionable tales. He told her that one time in the wilderness, he fell and couldn't get up. Wolves appeared and began circling. After struggling to get up, they backed off a bit. He said that as long as he was on his feet, the wolves wouldn't attack, but they would begin to close in if he faltered. While the wolves howled and paced back and forth, a punishing snowstorm began to bury his legs. Having thought the wolves were his friends all these years, he was incensed. He finally got upright, blustered curses at the wolves' deceptions and imperiously waved a stick. The sheepish wolves slinked off and Haines dragged himself home.

"To live out there you gotta be tough," Don Lee said. "Really, Haines was one of those odd ones, in the middle of godforsaken nowhere. If you pick a dot in the middle of nothin', that's where he'd live," Lee went on. "Usually someone like that is escaping something, like ex-wife or the law."

One day while delivering supplies, Haines did what he considered the ultimate compliment. He bestowed upon Kitty three beautiful martens he had trapped for a nice fur muffler. He recommended she take them to any native woman, who would know how to tan the hide. Kitty didn't know what to do with the beautiful sables, so she put them in the freezer. Apparently, one is not supposed to freeze whole dead animals. Her friend, famous mountaineer Jeff Lowe, volunteered to try to skin one. But the fur had become soggy and mangy - so a fur muffler was not to be. Even so, Kitty was grateful to Old Man Haines for his thoughtful gesture.

C180 47X in the early morning light

Kitty's Diary:

Autumn 1976. As Jim and I were departing from a delivery to Mr. Haines, an SOS came over the radio. Two men were asking for help after smashing their aircraft into the trees at a nearby lake. A portion of the lake iced up over the previous night. During takeoff, the mens plane had skimmed onto the ice and careened into the trees. Both men had survived the crash, but they were injured and there was no one else in the area to respond to their mayday.

We quickly flew to the scene of the accident and circled overhead. I could see tracks in the slush circling the downed airplane's tail, which stuck out of the woods with its frosted white trees. It was obviously unsafe to land on the lake, so we searched the area for another landing site, to no avail. We radioed the victims and I transmitted, "Are you guys okay to hike to another location?"

It was not the question the exhausted men wanted to hear, but they realized we were trying to help and making every effort to rescue them. There was silence on their part until a weak voice asked, "How far?"

Jim Sharp relayed the directions, estimating that it would take the men a full 24 hours to hike to the site where we had a chance to land to pick them up. Interested in saving their radio batteries, the men double-clicked a response and we flew off.

After all the circling and radio communication, the sky began darkening with the coming of twilight and we were pressured to land. We flew around for quite a while, searching for any water that was still in liquid form, and decided to head for a place Jim called the Farewell area. The name itself was a bit ominous. I knew nothing about the area, nor was it very familiar to Jim. But he'd heard of a large lake there and thought it would probably get enough wind action to keep it free of ice.

By the time we arrived on scene, the light was almost gone. We descended carefully and, up until our floats touched down, we didn't know whether the surface was going to have light ice. It was relieving to find that the lake was open water and on the shoreline an active camp.

A German woman, Marta, the wife of a well-known big game hunter, was commanding the kitchen and we couldn't have been luckier. It was like walking into Christmas. We stepped up into a beautiful log building equipped with a generator for electrical power. Fur hides hung like thick tapestries on the walls and from the ceilings and a large wooden table stood in the center of the room. While warm, fragrant moose meat stew simmered on the stove, a native Alaskan woman took our coats while the German woman poured cups of coffee for us. Also arriving after a day's work out on the grounds was her husband, Stan, and their native Alaskan guide.

After a huge family-style dinner, they brought out a film projector and showed an old super-eight movie. We felt so welcomed! They completely opened the place for us, fed us, housed us for the night, and got us rolling the next morning.

The temperatures allowed the lake to remain navigable, and we left early to head for the prearranged area. Flying a small, tight grid pattern, we searched the ground in vain for the two survivors only to finally see a flare shot skyward just as we started to depart the area. Jim wagged the wings in response and began scanning for the safest possible water-landing site, which turned out to be a narrow lake that already had ice rimming its edges. He landed and coasted up to a ramshackle cabin at the lake's edge. It turned out to be a vacated old hunter's lair with bear boards that could have been more easily pried off the door had we a crowbar for leverage. We were able to find some wood and quickly went to work inside, dusting off an old wood stove so I could start a fire with some kindling. Jim found an axe and began chopping firewood, planning now to thaw the frigid cabin before setting out in search of the men.

Suddenly, that search came directly to us. The door burst open and one of the men dragged himself inside, still bleeding from his crash injuries. We immediately wrapped him in our coats and encouraged him to lie down near the warming stove on which we were boiling lake water. He was completely dehydrated and sorely in need of water for drinking and for cleansing his wounds.

We asked him about his companion and were told his buddy stepped into the river, which had nearly frozen his feet making it extremely difficult to walk. The man was desperately forging on. We found him relatively close to the cabin and carried him inside to set him on one of the bunks. I then heated up canned beans and Spam that I found stashed in the cupboard.

I was still a newcomer to Alaska, and that night felt strange and long. I didn't sleep well, restless with an eerie feeling of being in the middle of nowhere and left with the nagging wonder whether we could ever get out. The cabin was warming, but the temperatures outside were dropping again and we were concerned the lake might ice over. Everything was quiet as the exhausted men slept soundly while Jim got up occasionally to stoke the glowing fire.

*Fairview Bar,
Village Airstrip, short final*

Unfortunately, advection fog crept in silently in the early morning to virtually mask the lake from sight. There was no way to predict that we wouldn't be marooned for a dangerously long period of time. It was difficult to know when, if ever, we were going to be able to fly to Talkeetna.

While we watched and waited, the insulating fog suddenly dissipated. We rushed to get the men roused and carried to the aircraft. We hurried through the courtesy of hammering the bear boards back onto the door. We needed to leave immediately to beat the rapid onset of light rime icing that licked at the lakeshore and threatened to spread quickly, cutting off our escape. As we settled the wounded men in the rear of the floatplane, I willed the ice on Windy Lake to give us time to get these fellows to the medical help they required in Talkeetna.

We were pretty heavily loaded, yet we powered onto the step, took off, and climbed over nearby trees to zoom through Rainy Pass. We reached town without further incident. This was my welcome to the world of rescue piloting in Alaska's unforgiving and unpredictable weather. It was truly 'Adventure Flying.'

Kitty and Sharp were skirting the town of Talkeetna and flew over the confluence of the three rivers; the waters frothing over rocks, limbs and tree roots. Tall, leafy black cottonwoods towered over other trees and brush, outlining the winding paths of the lush waterways – the rivers Chulitna, Talkeetna, and the "Big Su," the Susitna. From altitude, it was easy to see how Talkeetna thrived because of her rivers. They defined Talkeetna's setting, slaked its parched ground in times of drought and represented food and transportation for its inhabitants.

Flying over in the floatplane, Sharp pointed out a single, narrow, tree-lined grass and gravel runway, the Talkeetna Village Strip, (AK44), 1,600 x 30 feet, that ran perpendicular to the only paved road, Talkeetna's Main Street. This strip was the hanger base of Talkeetna Air Taxi.

High glacier, Jim Sharp photo

Sharp rocked his wings and they turned away from town and toward Christiansen Lake where he had left his parked truck. There, the floatplane would have a landing area near today's Alaska Floats and Skis, a bush piloting training base owned and operated by Don Lee. She watched intently as Sharp swung the aircraft into position for landing, applied flaps, and gently settled onto the still lake surface. They climbed out, secured the aircraft, unloaded their belongings, and reloaded Sharp's pickup to head back to the village airstrip they had just flown over. As they drew to a rolling stop in front of a large, silvery, steel building, Sharp said, "Welcome to your new home, yours and dozens of others, depending on the mountaineering crowd."

Don Sheldon built the big silver hangar just off the village airstrip. He'd designed the hangar with a large mechanized door and numerous large windows lining the top of the walls all around so natural light poured in. Now, Sharp was renting it from Roberta Sheldon. Within minutes, Kitty was unpacking for the second time, moving into a new space and getting acquainted with a home away from home.

A mosquito net protected a mattress on a platform in one corner of the hangar, and although no shower was installed, the bathroom had a sink with running water which allowed hands and faces to be washed and teeth to be brushed. Showers were across the street at Gene and Rose Jenny's Three Rivers Union 76 gas station, where you purchased tokens that would buy three minutes of (hopefully) warm water spray in the communal showers.

Jim Sharp wrote in his article, "Glacier Driving," "Much of being a pilot is dull, repetitive, hard work; for every hour in the air you must spend two on the ground, loading the airplane, fueling, cleaning the windshield, and filling out paperwork. And then afterwards, when the days began to shorten and the glacier flying slows down, there's always good ol' hunting season. I never could get rid of that slightly rancid smell in the plane."

One of the ways that the pilots endured the monotony of paperwork and routine maintenance was by spending their shared downtime together in the hangar. Early on, Sharp duly warned Kitty not to expect much privacy. The hangar had long been a popular meeting space for individuals, groups of climbers, skiers, fishermen and hunters. It was especially busy during the season between March through July when numerous expeditions aimed for Denali. Depending upon the weather, the building would be filled with upwards of 30 people, buzzing with a cacophony of different languages and laughter generated by those seeking to challenge Denali and reach its breathtaking heights. Sharp called it 'Talkeetna's largest living room." The space reeked of propane, avgas and heavyweight oil, or when the hangar doors were opened, the pungent cleansing odors of tamarack, hemlock, juniper and spruce carried in on the breeze.

The hangar still stands today after being moved to the Talkeetna State Airport. It is one of the few full-sized hangars in Alaska that enables mechanics to work in natural light. Its massive doors are fully mechanized for easy access of airplanes getting in and out, yet to live in it was another story.

Jim Sharp later wrote, "Ah, hangar living, 3,000 square feet with nary an interior wall. It was really like camping out in the gymnasium of the local high school after a hurricane, flood or an earthquake. No one believed we actually lived there, so they didn't hesitate to barge in - clients wanting to be ferried somewhere late at night, town folks thinking we were up late tinkering with the planes."

Talkeetna is known for inventing several world-famous events, such as the Bachelors Ball and Wilderness Women's Contest. In the contest, ladies compete by chopping wood, lugging large buckets of frozen water, charging snowmobiles over obstacles like river overflow, shooting at a target and then they have to assemble a sandwich with an instruction from a local bachelor who happens to be sitting in a recliner with the fake TV remote control. It was also known for its popular Moose Dropping Festival, the weekend after the 4th of July. One of the activities of the Moose Dropping Festival consisted of all the local pilots performing a formation flyby together over the people.

In the mid to late 1970s, competition was stiff. Rivalries abounded and accusations flew on who stole whose paying client. But yearly, the pilots would swallow their pride to do the formation flyby together over the annual Talkeetna festival.

TKA, Kitty & Old Sourdough, Miner's Day, 1976

Rocky Cummins' 90th. Kitty, Sharron Bushell, Rocky, & Kathy Sullivan

Part of the not-so-friendly competition in town amidst pilots included the daily "scalping" at the train station. "It was a scene right out of an airport in Mexico," Kitty remembered. Climbers, easy to spot in their brightly colored parkas, would arrive to begin their climbing adventure. "The pilots would approach them, pointing toward the mountain, simulating airplane wings with their arms, gesturing that we could fly them up to Denali," she said. This worked well since many arriving climbers did not speak English.

"Mostly, you wanted to be there to make sure your customers weren't snagged," Mike Fisher explained.

Kitty and her friend, Kathy Sullivan, would drive their trucks up to the train station, and on one occasion, Kathy spotted a particularly good-looking French climber dressed in a hot pink one-piece running suit and walked up to him. She quietly grabbed his gear, loaded it in her truck and drove off. The climber turned out to be a famous European extreme skier. He'd already pre-paid his flight with another air taxi, which had been searching all over town for him, yet Kathy's hospitality trumped his pre-paid transportation.

"Yeah, we were definitely friendly competitors," Don Lee agreed. "That's back when I did *Bandido* work. I was uninsured, unrated, and I'd pass the savings on to the customer," he laughed.

Kitty was getting a feel for the air taxi experience and falling in love with Talkeetna with its unique visitors and their eclectic collection of languages, habits, stories, and talents. She crossed paths with friendly trappers and miners, the "old timers" of Talkeetna, like Jim Beaver and Rocky Cummings, who were still so active in their later years of life. Ken Holland of Holland Air Service noted that one of the joys of discovery in moving to Alaska was in meeting these distinctive, rugged individualists. They offered a direct connection with the town's roots in gold mining, hunting and fur trapping and brought authenticity to the stories of the early days of Talkeetna.

Early on, Sharp formally introduced her to Roberta Sheldon and her children, Holly, Kate, and Robert. Kitty was amazed by the display of Don Sheldon's memorabilia on their living room wall, yet she knew the wounds of having lost her husband must be tragically raw. She respected Roberta's stature in the town as she negotiated the many demands upon her time and her legitimate desire for privacy. Kitty felt very fortunate to form a relationship of trust from the outset of meeting her as the two became close friends. Roberta would drop by the hangar in the evenings to say hello and visit. Kitty welcomed chances to watch over Holly, Kate and Robert when

Roberta had to be away traveling the Aleutian Islands, as liaison for Reeve Aleutian Airways, founded by her father, Robert (Bob) Campbell Reeve. In a journal entry that May, Kitty wrote, "BATH at Sheldons, house sitting one hamster, two mice, one large rabbit, one feisty goose, one parrot, a white dove and Lady, her dog!"

Sharp also made a point of introducing Kitty to Suzanne Guimaraes and Mike Fisher, who lived not far from the hangar on the village airstrip. They invited her into their recently built two-story frame home. Suzanne, a graduate of Cornell University, had come to the area to work as a hand at Milton Litenwalner's farm. In Talkeetna, the couple enjoyed building a cabin, vegetable gardening, hiking, biking and spending quiet time reading.

Suzanne in her vegetable garden

The first time she met them, Suzanne served Kitty tea in their upstairs living room and launched into a wonderful series of questions, wanting to know all about her. Suzanne, who was later Talkeetna's postmistress, was also a master gardener. In the long hours of daylight of the Alaskan growing season, she raised vegetables that grew to tremendous sizes. Kitty would come to spend afternoons with Suzanne in that bright upper room, drinking tea and eating wraps of scrambled eggs and an English muffin rolled in a giant lettuce leaf from her garden.

Her partner, Mike Fisher, was the town inventor. Michigan born, Fisher traveled to Alaska in 1962, just out of the army and up for a little adventure. He first worked as an aircraft mechanic in Anchorage, then moved on to Talkeetna and became friends with Don Sheldon, at Talkeetna Air Service. Fisher eventually doubled as both a pilot and mechanic, working for Sheldon Air Service for several years. On the first floor of their two-story frame home, Fisher operated the Talkeetna Machine Shop, a state-of-the-art workshop where he hand created beautifully machined parts. He was both an artist and an engineer and he spoke like a professor of mechanical engineering. Stacked carefully in every nook and cranny of the shop was a vast magazine collection, a broad-based wealth of knowledge from which to draw. He had an uncanny sense of humor. His sister, Margot, said that he derived great enjoyment in helping other people solve their problems. Sometimes that meant working pro bono, but that was okay with Fisher. One of the many works he designed and built was his own portable log mill. Fisher was the quintessential bush pilot and an excellent flight instructor. He also built his own indigenous log cabin.

Kitty was elated when Fisher agreed to take her on as a student and prepare her for glacier landings and a commercial flight certificate. She wrote, "In all, I would name Mike, with his excellence in flight instruction, as the most important person in my Alaskan aviation career."

Fisher had an extensive knowledge of aerodynamics, mechanics, and aircraft performance. He encouraged sound judgment, which coupled with the expertise Kitty had learned from Dave Rahm, equipped her for handling bush and glacier flights with confidence. But training with Fisher for her commercial certificate (and the legal right to carry passengers for money) had to wait for the next flying season. Winter pushed its icy fingers along the rivers, amid the trees, and into every corner of the cold silver hangar. Snow flurries teased and those who lived in town full time knew deep snows and long, dark days would follow.

Sharp and Kitty flew the C180 floatplane to Lake Hood in Anchorage to help Roger Boer, the mechanic, convert it from floats to wheels. Suddenly, as if the October weather needed to assert itself, more than a foot of snow dumped on the town. Cold saturated Talkeetna and heralded the dark, frigid season ahead. Kitty's short introduction to Talkeetna Air Taxi was coming to an end. With the winter of 1976-1977 lurking in the wings, she had to wait until spring to taste the thrill of her first glacier landing.

That winter, Sharp invited Kitty to co-pilot the high-performance Cessna 185 from Alaska to Mexico via Montana and Colorado. He suggested they stop on the return to see a friend, artist Stanley Marsh, at his ranch in Amarillo, Texas. Kitty had met Marsh in Talkeetna and knew about his half-buried, paint-splattered Cadillacs adorning the desert. She was enthusiastic about visiting Marsh's Texas studio and perhaps seeing what sort of contribution to pop art he was contemplating. Best of all, she was facing the opportunity to experience Mexico with a pilot who was raised in Mexico City and who knew the country well.

Her only experience south of the border was an Acapulco trip with her family, but she could certainly recall its beauty. El Mirador Hotel where the Banner family stayed, had beautiful views of the quiet Santa Lucia Bay and a dramatic view of the Pacific Ocean beating against the base of the stark and rugged cliffs of La Quebrada. Now she had a chance to fly throughout the region at her own pace, and she was with a man whose command of the Spanish language was truly admirable. Being a writer, poet and photographer, she knew the trip to Mexico with him was going to be memorable.

Kitty studied the airway charts to familiarize herself with the routes that lie ahead. They plotted a route south and southeast from Talkeetna along a path following the Alcan Highway to Whitehorse in the Yukon Territory and across the Tundra Pipeline and the Alaska Range through the trench. Considering weight and balance, she packed only necessities. They took along a baggage compartment loaded with the treat that most in the lower 48 rarely tasted: moose meat-cut, packaged and frozen.

Kitty had taken dual training in the high-performance Cessna 185, the 'Skywagon' six-place, single-engine workhorse of the Cessna fleet. Day one of the trip, the Mackenzie Mountains rose to join the Rockies in the distance off their left wing, but the view didn't last long. Wintry fog and mist quickly hid the treachery of the mountain peaks and she and Sharp maintained altitudes that guaranteed adequate separation from the hidden menace.

The two pilots traded shifts at the controls between Whitehorse and Watson Lake. They stopped for fuel and some food at Fort Nelson, British Columbia, intending to press on. The weather closed in and they couldn't leave Fort Nelson until the following morning. The next day, they left British Columbia and headed for Dawson Creek and Grand Prairie in Alberta. They had nothing but time, the ability to travel and the wide expanse of mountains and valleys stretching as far as they could see.

Heading south from Grand Prairie, they passed over the huge dam in Revelstoke in Canada's Glacier National Park that harnessed the mighty Columbia River near its source. They bypassed the popular tourist sites of Banff, Calgary and Lake Louise, and as they crossed from Canada into Montana, they reveled in the beauty of the lustrous aquamarine waters of Waterton Lakes National Park and Glacier National Park. Beneath them was the famed *Going to the Sun Highway*, a 52-mile paved road that twisted and snaked among jagged snow-dusted peaks.

Landing in Great Falls, Montana, they borrowed a car at the airport and stayed with a friend, storing the moose meat in his freezer for the night. The next day, they flew over Lewis and Clark National Forest and the rolling wheat fields of Montana, descending to cross Custer National Forest and finally landing at Red Lodge Airport. As are many mountain airports, Red Lodge is hewn from a mountain ridge at almost a 6000-foot elevation while the town itself is located hundreds of feet below in a stream-fed valley.

As they settled toward Red Lodge Airport, smoke billowed from the chimneys of wood-burning stoves warming the homes 200 feet below. Dark clouds swelled and churned from the basin as if from a steaming pot. Wood smoke filtered into their cockpit with the unmistakable aromas that warmed the night, transporting them to happy hours spent around the fire with their Montana climbing friends, Jim Kanzler and Jack Tackle.

The next morning, as the aircraft crossed the mountains at Laramie, Wyoming, on its way to Denver, the weather started deteriorating. It was a challenging spot. The regional airport, at 7000 feet, boasts one of the lowest passes for pilots selecting a flight route over the Rocky Mountains. They pressed on. As the promise of favorable weather reports manifested, it became a sort of "scud running" around Colorado's Estes Park. Scud running, which means to dip beneath low ceilings and hope to keep the aircraft out of clouds, hail, rain, turbulence, and most importantly, the granite known to exist in those clouds in mountainous terrain, can prove to be dangerous at best and fatal at worst.

Recognizing the Flatirons and Estes Park in the murk, they knew Boulder's welcoming airport was just ahead. Upon reaching familiar surroundings, they landed at the Boulder Airport after having flown 18.4 hours over seven days. After unloading cargo, they stashed the moose meat in a refrigerated meat locker and sorted out plans to return months later. Before nightfall, they went separate directions to visit friends and family.

In February, Kitty and Sharp met back at the Boulder hangar to fly to Mexico. They loaded the Cessna 185 with their gear, topped off the fuel, checked the weather and took off toward Chihuahua, Mexico. From Boulder, it was a five and a half hour flight. Over the course of several weeks, they landed in astonishing landscapes and encountered unexpected expressions of humanity. As they flew over the skies of Mexico, each of their landings was another encounter with a spectacular moment in time and space, another tiny miracle.

One of their surprise landings was in the middle of a banana plantation just before dark. They tipped the night watchman, an old guy wearing a borrowed military jacket, to roll up in blankets and spend the night beneath the aircraft while they secured the prop with a lock and chain to ensure the airplane would still be in the same place in the morning. They landed on beaches, grass strips and a few well-tended airports.

The duo skirted spectacular ancient Mayan ruins and took opportunities to visit some outstanding sites, fascinated to witness the crumbling remains of a formerly brilliant, flourishing culture in which a new war was being fought; the recapture and destruction of centuries-old buildings by the voracious jungle with its creeping vines and tenacious undergrowth.

Kitty and Sharp saw sculptured serpents, their heads pressed flat upon the ground and tails reaching toward the clouds. To the ancient Mayans, the serpent symbolized a celestial life force, bringing rain and connecting the body and earth with the sky and all spiritual aspirations.

They ate in little old palapas with dirt floors, as cheerful women stirred stews, the clay pots bubbling, orbited by pesky flies. At those outdoor cafes, Kitty felt as if she could travel anywhere. She considered heading to the Palenque, where she could reconnect with missionary pilots like the ones headed for Ethiopia whom she had met in Bellingham.

The next stop was Alamos, a historic town in the Sierra Madre Mountains. El Cárcel, a jail being remodeled into a cultural center, was particularly interesting. It was perched high on Guadalupe Hill and offered an excellent viewpoint to look down on the city.

From Alamos, the flight via Mazatlán took them south along Mexico's western coast for a brief lunch stop at Puerto Vallarta. Next up was Barra de Navidad, Jalisco, near Manzanillo, arriving at sunset to a memorable kaleidoscope of color. A flowing mix of blood red and golden sunbeams swirled as the orb lowered slowly into the Pacific Ocean. They touched down as gently as they could on the dirt strip, as if to keep from disturbing nature's incredible display.

That evening they were invited to join new acquaintances at "Carlos y Amigos, a discotheque on the bay," Kitty noted in her diary. Like guitars and maracas, waves pounded characteristic Latin musical rhythms. A day later after a swim, she added, "Y la langosta para desayuno, we flew the short 45-minute flight to Guadalajara. We returned to Barra de Navidad to shoot landings and takeoffs."

Her dream of becoming more accomplished at the controls of a tailwheel-equipped aircraft was coming true. Repeated practice and success with the taildragger handling characteristics resulted in improvements in her timing, spatial orientation, aircraft control and confidence. As the trip unfolded, each flight introduced vivid and unbelievably glorious scenes that flash to mind with nothing more to jog her memory than a simple glance at her diary and the margins of her logbooks.

Sharp and Kitty flew direct Barra de Navidad to the airport at Ciudad Ixtepec, Oaxaca, near Tehuantepec. They passed the famed tourist destination, the resort she and her family had visited in Acapulco, and banked to circle a few times and snap a few pictures. The weather allowed for a good view of the stretches of sand, surf and the rising terrain of the Sierra Madre del Sur. They pressed on to the isthmus of the Gulf of Tehuantepec that connects southern Mexico with the Yucatan Peninsula and with Guatemala.

With each passing day, she grew more appreciative of the geography lessons and the rich experiences she was enjoying. She reveled in the travel and the wide variety of serendipitous meetings that took her breath away.

Kitty's Diary:

Ciudad Ixtepec: We met a pilot and mechanic, Mike Sullivan, and his Swiss passenger. He works on Jacque Cousteau's PBY and other aircraft currently around Costa Rica. Mike chuckled and explained, "It's handy to have at the ready seven professional French divers to retrieve the tools that invariably slip out of my hands into the deep-sea water."

We were having trouble obtaining the 100-octane fuel we required. Sharp and I joined forces with Mike and his passenger, who had been waiting for promised fuel for three days, and parked our aircraft together for the night. It made a bit of a statement and, finally, on Sunday morning 'El Jefe' made 100-octane gas available to us out of 55-gallon drums.

The two took off on February 13 to fly to Tuxtla Gutiérrez, the capital city of Chiapas.

Again, it was compelling to see the historic buildings and to experience the sounds, sights and spicy odors wafting from markets, restaurants and opened windows. The pleasure of exchanging smiles, nods and appreciation of the locals was surpassed only by the marvelous architecture in towns we visited and those we managed to explore.

Not far from the city, we saw the ruins of an ancient Mayan ceremonial center, the Chiapa de Corzo, with stone platforms and terraced pyramids. Each structure was topped by ancient and haunting temple, dramatically contrasting with today's thatched adobe hut, vegetables growing from the thick dirt-covered roof and space for domestic animals to live inside with the people.

Pushing on, the two flew past an impressive canyon, Cañon del Sumidero, and Kitty couldn't help but think of her brother John and how much he would enjoy mountain climbing amid the rugged crags. From Tuxtla and in Mexico's Chiapas, Sharp and Kitty reached as close to the Guatemala border as San Cristóbal de las Casas on Valentine's Day. Kitty's diary noted some time spent relaxing in a spa, a Baña Vapor, at El Español Hotel and that she and Sharp connected with more friends, Sheila, John and Mara. It was "Muy Bueno!"

Early the next morning, she took a walk to take photographs of the city. The ruins of Palenque are grand and glorious reminders of the lofty realms of the Mayan culture. It boasts several temples topping ancient pyramids, and dates to Mexico's Classic Era believed to have existed between 400 and 700 AD. One pyramid, inextricably enveloped in dense jungle, houses the tomb of a mighty Mayan ruler, Pakal the Great. Incredibly, it was as recent as 1952 before archaeologists discovered the roughly-hewn, steep, 80-foot stairway that leads down to Pakal's tomb.

As close as they were to Guatemala and the Yucatan Peninsula, they discovered that if they were to continue, the insurance policy covering the aircraft would be invalid. Furthermore, Palenque was struck with some of the torrential downpours for which the area is famous. Their plans had to change.

In San Cristóbal de las Casas, they went to the local outdoor market and bought colorful handmade woven tapestries and then flew across the isthmus to Oaxaca. Liberally decorating her diary entries with drawings of balloons, palm trees, gulls, ocean waves, a shining sun, and numerous mountain peaks, it read like an illustrated tourist guidebook with exotic names and places listed among her joyful quixotic miniature drawings. She noted, "We went everywhere and, from Oaxaca, our next stop was Mexico City, where Jim's father lived."

In late February, Kitty wrote in her diary, "Flew with a Mexican 'narc' pointing out marijuana and poppy fields." One day later, she added, "We spent time with Jim's father and celebrated Señor Sharp's cumpleanos."

Senior Sharp was enthusiastic about the city he called his own and encouraged his son and Kitty to make sure they appreciated the centuries-old heritage, as well as its respected home to more than 20 million.

Kitty's Diary:

We ate in an old convent and garden, the San Angel Inn, and explored bustling Mexico City, and, a day later, we lunched in the garden at Garibaldi Square, and were delighted by mariachi music played by musicians dressed in Charro costumes. We danced in the street to the toe-tapping, hip-swaying music of trumpets, violins, guitars and bass guitars.

They flew to lunch at Las Mañanitas in Cuernavaca and descended to sea level to take on fuel in Manzanillo. It was time to return from the tropics and Kitty was eager to head north. Kitty took the controls in Manzanillo and wrote, "I made three touch and goes on the beach and buzzed into Barra de Navidad."

Sharp and Kitty pointed the Cessna 185 north for Stanley Marsh's ranch, landing nearby in Amarillo, Texas. The wealthy and outgoing Marsh was famous for his pop-art culture. He famously contributed to the Ant Farm of San Francisco and built his Cadillac Ranch abreast of a stretch of historic Route 66.

Kitty's Diary:

Before landing, we flew over the ranch to view the cars for which the ranch is named. In a bizarre homage to the Golden Age of American Automobiles from 1949 through 1963, Marsh 'planted' ten wildly painted Cadillacs like so many angled fruit trees, seeking a maximum advantage from the sun. The cars were buried nose first into the sandy soil, their characteristic and familiar fins sticking up into the air.

In another display, recognizable only from the air, his property was outlined on the ground in the shape of an enormous pool table complete with billiard balls and a cue stick. After parking and tying down the aircraft, a big, long, black, stretch limo rolled up to the terminal building. Marsh's driver had hair pulled back into a long ponytail that reached below his belt. We climbed into the rear seats and rode off. At the Toad Hall Ranch, the limo passed a huge water tower. It was a replica of a can of Campbell's soup but the lettering said 'Marshmallow Soup'.

His house was pretty bizarre and hard to describe. In the living room a beautiful, small, sport airplane hanging from the ceiling. Immediately adjacent to the indoor room was an outdoor area housing a variety of stalls for a tattooed pig bearing wings on each haunch, a zebra, another exotic animal - perhaps a yak, and several llamas. Maybe he wanted to breed a cow to a yak and result in a Cattle-Yak?

The pantry and kitchen held multiple products, carefully arranged, Peter Max style. Instead of one box of Tide, there were six boxes. Rather than one container of Joy dishwashing liquid, there were eight. The house was extremely colorful - primarily deep oranges and blues - and everything, it seemed to me, was artistically designed and placed.

A year later, when Marsh had introduced his group to Alaska in 1977, Kitty was told they had boated down the Amazon River the year prior, all dressed as native South American Indians. In Alaska, they wore authentic Boy Scout uniforms and one of them carried a shiny brass bugle. They were transported up to the 7,200-foot base camp of Mt. McKinley, landed on the glacier and as Marsh said, "to hike down the mountain instead of hiking up." They stomped around a bit to the bugler's beat and were then flown back to TKA. While they were on the mountain, Kitty searched for a recipe that would suffice for worldly travelers. As she was living in the hangar and limited to her three-burner Coleman Stove, any dinner prepared was similarly limited. Kitty wondered what kind of a meal she could make in a skillet that would be interesting and came upon a recipe in *The Sourdough Book*. Kitty and her friend, Cyndi, went to work to follow the directions and none of them ever forgot that the guests received the local special: Upside Down Moosemeat Pie. Somehow, it seemed fitting.

A bush pilot was awakening in Kitty. She could hardly wait to get to the wild north to try her wings and test new skills. With the climbing season ahead, Talkeetna, Alaska would still be in the throes of ice break-up and winter's reluctant thaw.

Super Cub on Glacier

Mexican security guard

Remote runway, Mexico trip in C185

Stanley Marsh & his Scouts,TKA

Stanley Marsh Troop,
Jim Sharp photo

CHAPTER SEVEN

Adventure

T en years after the Wright brothers succeeded with powered flight, the year 1913 recorded the first mountaineering climb to reach a summit of Mt. McKinley (now Denali) with four men setting foot on the South Summit, an achievement that laid the groundwork for the thousands who subsequently have chosen the arduous goal of summiting some of the most breathtaking of the planet's highest elevations.

"One practices the art of adventure when [she] has the daring to open doors to new experiences and to step boldly forth to explore strange horizons,... unafraid of new ideas, new theories, and new philosophies; Keeps [her] heart young and expectations high and never allows dreams to die."

—Peterson

Two decades later, a fearless Alaskan dared take a powered craft to the surface of a glacier. That gutsy trailblazer was Joe Crosson, who in April 1932, was reputed to be the first to land an aircraft on the Muldrow Glacier near the 5,700-foot McGonagall Pass. He was followed by Bob Reeve, the Alaskan bush pilot based out of Valdez on Prince William Sound who was the first to make glacier landings a successful business.

Reeve, a ski-plane pioneer, developed a method for glacier landings. Bradford Washburn hired Reeve for his 1937 ascent of Mt. Luciana in the Yukon. Fifteen years later, Washburn asked Reeve for the name of a pilot who could fly him onto glaciers in the Alaska Range. He introduced Don Sheldon and together they made a long-time career flying the glaciers of Mt. McKinley. By 1954, Don Sheldon made history with the first commercial flight from Talkeetna to land on the Kahiltna Glacier.

Washburn, the ardent cartographer who mapped the mountain and was the first to demonstrate the route to the West Buttress, most taken by climbers today, opened the continent's highest mountain to climbers.

Michael Sfraga notes that in 1939, "Washburn was the first person to scale Mt. McKinley three times, complete the first aerial photographic survey of the mountain, and produce the authoritative map of the peak."

It is significant, that Washburn's wife, Barbara, became the first woman to summit the great mountain, making them a true mountaineering couple.

Roberta Sheldon & Super Cub 23Z

Roberta Sheldon wrote in her *The Heritage of Talkeetna*: "In the mid-1950s, aviation grew more sophisticated with the availability of retractable aircraft skis, which aviator Don Sheldon immediately purchased for his high performance Super Cub, one of four aircraft operated by Talkeetna Air Service. The ability to takeoff from the village airstrip on wheels, and on skis where late snows lingered, provided the opportunity to extend the season for flights to the high country. Every paying flight counted. Then, a chance to earn some really substantial

*Kitty & Roberta
flying her Super Cub 23Z*

revenue presented itself with the appearance of Dr. Washburn... [who] needed a pilot and ski-equipped aircraft that could devote a lot of time to transporting him to various glacier locations in the Alaska Range. Sheldon eagerly accepted and so began a career of glacier flying that would span the next two decades, mostly providing air support for hundreds of mountaineering expeditions that were intent upon testing themselves on McKinley and throughout the Alaska Range."

Rescuing members of the ill-fated John Day climb on May 20, 1960, Sheldon coaxed his 150-horsepower Super Cub to a landing at the incredible altitude of 14,300 feet on McKinley's West Buttress. Once it was known the feat had been accomplished, other glacier pilots challenged themselves to gain information about prevailing wind currents and the effects of mountain topography to master high altitude operations.

Doug Geeting at 14,300' in C185

Doug Geeting, with park ranger Nick Hartzell aboard, tested the performance of his Cessna 185 by successfully making a glacier landing at the lofty 14,300 foot mark in June 1976. Most pilots understand such feats to be above the service ceiling of non-turbocharged piston-powered engines, but, the need to perform a rescue and the ability to make superlative use of prevailing updrafts on the windward side of the mountain outweighed any published limitations in aircraft owners' manuals.

Don Sheldon represented two generations of Alaskan pilots: the early pioneers who demonstrated the potential of aviation to Alaskans and those of the modern phalanx who swept flying to its premier position at the forefront of Alaskan transportation. The timing of Kitty's arrival positioned her between early Alaskan aviation and its contemporary role. Everyone who had known Sheldon had a firsthand account to share with her. Mike Fisher and Lynn Twigg shared their flying stories that gave her a wellspring of information to absorb and digest. They told of Sheldon's uncanny knowledge of weather systems, his amazing talents as a pilot and his ability to "read" the topography and orient himself in dangerously cloudy or turbulent conditions with even the briefest glimpse of the terrain. Those who had witnessed or been involved in a rescue composed a legion of fans, all of whom held him, justifiably, as a legend.

Just as she had been inspired by Don Sheldon, Bob Reeve, Cliff Hudson, Lynn Twigg, Mike Fisher, and other successful aviation pioneers, Kitty and her contemporaries composed the modern sect of committed pilots who demonstrated the basic qualities of piloting boldness and enterprise initiated with the pioneers. With Jim Sharp, Doug Geeting, Lowell Thomas, Jr., Jay Hudson, Kimball Forrest, Ed Homer, Jim Okonek, Don Lee, Tony Martin, and later David Lee and Paul Roderick, she joined the new generation of Alaskan pilots.

Spring in Alaska brought both delight and challenge. As darkness gave way to ethereal sunshine, flowers and tundra grasses reached for the promised light and warmth. Denali sits in Denali National Park, but the Park Service is not in the business of ferrying climbers on and off the mountain. Talkeetna pilots ferry the climbers, along with doing search and rescue, cargo delivery, transport sightseers which have become flightseers when an airplane is involved, and the endless list of helpful transportation that falls under the heading of customer service.

On April 15, 1977, Kitty arrived in Anchorage and Sharp picked her up in the Cessna 185 on wheel skis, then flying them directly to The Mountain House on the Ruth Glacier. Kitty, dressed in jeans, her Eddie Bauer corduroy sport jacket, and clogs, found herself stepping out of the airplane onto deep snow in cold temperatures. She wasn't exactly dressed for the occasion. She pulled a down jacket, hat, gloves,

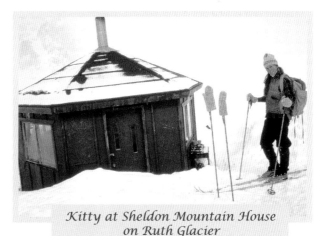

Kitty at Sheldon Mountain House on Ruth Glacier

Kitty repairing the wheel-ski flat tire on Cub

Kitty fueling from a 55-gallon drum

Sheldon crew wash Kimball's C180

and boots from her pack to replace her travel clothing and prepared to ski up to the Sheldon Mountain House. Spending the night and waking to find the weather had closed in, they skied down to the plane to pick up more wood that was stashed there and ferried it back up. The next day, the weather lifted, the sky cleared and they flew back to the hangar at the village airstrip.

Kitty was happy to be back in Talkeetna and returned to her familiar makeshift bed under mosquito netting, the small kitchen area with a Coleman stove along the wall and the plywood desk balancing on two sawhorses. An airplane was parked in the 'living room' along with her bicycle, leaning on the wall.

"She's very refined, but could muck down with the best of 'em," Lee laughed. "If the truck got stuck she'd be right in there pulling it out. She was grace under fire. I don't think anybody really taught her how to fly up there. She just sort of absorbed it."

Kate Sheldon remembered, "When Kitty arrived back in Talkeetna in early spring, she was instantly enchanted with the old timers who lingered in front of the B & K Trading Post recalling their Gold Rush days and sharing memories of a challenging yesteryear. Depending upon the time of day, the weather and activities affecting the town, the old timers would be fully engaged in one another's stories of escapades they'd shared and repeated interminably or stories concocted to make one another laugh or slap their knees in glee."

Kitty was treated royally by the elderly gents who nobody had paid attention to in years, who according to Don Lee, "Would out of respect tip their hats as she walked past." When it was suggested that everyone who met Kitty fell in love with her, Lee retorted with a broad smile, "What's not to love?"

He was far from alone. Kate wrote about her, "Radiating a smile that sparkled more brightly than the snow on a clear day. Men tried to court her and girls wanted to be like her."

In addition to the old-timers, Kitty enjoyed the company of contemporaries, whom Kate Sheldon described as "a new breed of mavericks who, whether trappers, miners, climbers, hunters, fishermen, scientists, artists or woodsmen, were apt to be part of those no longer tethered to the earth; but able to take to the air. Since early in the 20th century, an aircraft was a novel, life-changing device. With Denali within sight, people in Talkeetna sought the best way to access

*Don Lee, moose antlers,
Stephan Lake*

*Kate Sheldon &
Sheldon Super Cub 23Z*

views of the majestic massif and were hard-pressed to find more accommodating, faster access to the tundra, woods, rivers and mountain ranges than in a reliable, well-piloted aircraft."

Don Lee was one such airman. He arrived a few years before Kitty at age 17. He was drawn from Minnesota to the great land because it was the last frontier. An enthusiastic and strong kid, he was one of the crewmembers who helped pack cargo; handling everything from tools, aircraft parts and oversized crates, to the freeze-packed fish of tourists or newly butchered carcasses of game hunters. Daily, Don slung heavy objects with an agility that belied their weight, all while working on his pilot certifications.

"I'd left the last day after high school graduation. I'd gotten Alaska magazine and was writing to the various outfitters who advertised in it in the hopes of a job," Lee remembered. "A fella, Nic Botner at Stephan Lake, wrote me back and soon I was helping him at this remote lake."

100

Lee guided, cooked, cleaned and did maintenance for the fly-in-only rustic resort for years. He became intrigued with flying. "A pilot said he'd show me how to fly, so I said, great! We took off the runway, playing the stall horn like a cheap flute and went straight into the trees," Lee said. "We wrecked upside down. A person who was waiting to fly out appeared and the first thing he asked was are we okay. The next thing he said was, 'You got grass?' He was one of those hippies that lived in the woods. Third thing he said was, 'Ah, shit. You're my ride out of here.'" So, went his first lesson in flying.

Don Lee could shoulder unbelievably heavy loads on his back. He could shoulder emotional loads, as well. As a teenager, Lee worked for a couple of years before hearing from his younger siblings, David and Jody, that they were following him to Alaska. They joined him in the bush and moved into a camper, a good-sized bus parked back in Talkeetna's woods that was little more than a rough shelter from storms, cold and bears.

Doug Geeting was another well-known Alaskan bush pilot who arrived in Anchorage from California in 1975 and on to Talkeetna in the spring of 1976 to fly for Cliff Hudson, Hudson Air Service. Doug earned his living flying the mountains of Alaska delivering mountain climbers, river rafters, gold miners, and tourists to the most remote parts of Alaska. He rarely landed on asphalt, touching down mostly on glaciers and river bars. Doug started Geeting Aviation in 1982. When he was not flying, Doug would play guitar at the local pubs. He had a distinctive sound with a deep baritone voice and would play a harp, 12-string and assorted 6-string guitars. He played with musicians such as Jimmy Buffett, John Denver and more as they traveled through Talkeetna.

When Kitty arrived in 1976, Doug helped her acquire the wisdom and knowledge she needed and was generous with good advice. In addition to encouraging safety in every glacier approach and landing, Doug impressed upon her the importance of taking stock. He insisted, "If in doubt, DON'T!" He believed it so ardently that he taped the warning on the control stick or yoke in each aircraft he flew. Kitty was always grateful for the many ways that Doug contributed to her life and they would remain close friends.

Although reticent to admit it, Kitty certainly received her share of male Talkeetna-style attention. Mike Fisher remembered, "She was completely appreciated and loved by the male pilots with whom she worked because they could tease her and get a laugh from her instead of a sharp response. Kitty was always looking for ways to share her love of flying with a diverse circle of friends," he recalled. "Many of them did not have money for highly structured training programs with standard category airplanes. Still, they learned to fly and would make large sacrifices to join in the adventure and freedom promised by aviation. One of them, Harold "Spike" Maness, had solved the cost problem by building an airplane and getting it licensed in the experimental category. It was a beautiful little open-cockpit, parasol-wing monoplane with a powerful engine. It wasn't long before Kitty was interested in flying it. She called me, her flight instructor who was helping her prepare for the commercial pilot practical test," Mike said with a smile, "and I had done some of the required test flying in the

Harold "Spike" Maness & C185

steep-climbing, highly-responsive sport plane and was quite fond of it, so I readily agreed to share the fun."

Mike admitted there was a problem. "The business end of the control stick was carved to feel and look like a fully erect male phallus. The airplane gang thought this was hilarious, but it wasn't so funny to me as I pondered the impression this whimsical touch might make. Kitty was high-spirited and fun loving, but also very much a lady. No coarse language or inappropriate remarks ever parsed her lips, even in times of danger or stress. I decided it would be okay to go ahead and make the flight. I made no attempt to change or mask the stick grip in any way, knowing she could handle dicey situations with grace and panache. I had seen her do so on quite a few occasions."

Fisher recalled that when Kitty seated herself in the airplane and noted the unorthodox grip, she simply remarked, "What an interesting... stick handle."

"She quickly adapted to the sensitive controls and touchy ground-handling of the experimental airplane and flew it with precision and grace."

Until she was fully qualified, Kitty flew virtually anywhere and everywhere to earn the experience. She flew between Talkeetna and Wasilla, where she shopped at the market within walking distance of the airport, and Anchorage, landing at Merrill Field for radio repairs, deliveries, or to pick up equipment. She

Mike Fisher & Kitty in Harold's homebuilt

Casey, Charlie, Scott, Cyndi, Kimball, & Lili

flew with some good friends who came to Talkeetna, Cyndi and Scott Thorburn, and took them on a local sight-seeing flight, one similar in yaw and roll to the twists and turns she flew with Ray "Pirate" Genet following the rivers to find downed logs suitable for peeling, scraping, fitting, and building into log cabins or a two-story office building for Genet Expeditions. She made the flights into familiarization rides with sweeping banks, steep and shallow turns, and by following the circuitous paths of the rivers, she pointed out special mountain peaks to give them a good vantage point from which to see Denali when it was visible in all its glory. By June 1977, her logbook showed that she'd accrued several hundred hours, worked on advanced ratings and had flown numerous passengers.

Kitty admitted the loading of the aircraft was tricky. From passengers, equipment, knapsacks, backpacks and sleeping bags, everything was stuffed in the back of the aircraft. As there was no cover or protection to keep the control cables free and clear, she was always concerned about sliding in long skis and heavy objects. To keep passengers from grabbing the back-seat stick, which controlled the ailerons and elevator, the roll and pitch of the craft, Kitty and other pilots removed the upper portion while the short end still existed and needed to move freely. There was no netting and you had to pack around it. She quickly discovered packing had to be done very carefully to make sure the control stick would not become jammed. Kitty often chose to put sleeping bags there because as opposed to a firm or a stiff object, if anything shifted, one could still get full control. She distinctly remembers most flights being way overloaded and packed to the roof, a common occurrence flying to remote locations.

In Alaska, weather conditions are paramount to the glacier pilot. Kitty was quickly learning that on any spring or summer day, chances of seeing Denali's peak were rare. Clouds form over the river-drained, moist lowlands, starting to build in the early morning and cooling as they rise to become a solid ceiling that might be 5,000 feet thick by evening. It was up to the pilot to find an opening, a hole in the clouds that would allow a safe descent to a vantage point, giving passengers views of the mountain.

In prepping for her first dual landing on the Kahiltna Glacier, Kitty flew the 45-mile long river of ice several times. From a bird's-eye view, she could feel it's cold allure and could easily locate climbers and their tents, confirm the locations of their base camps, and in spaced tethered lines to protect from falls into deep glacial crevasses. The climbers shown like tiny black ants scrambling up a monochromatic landscape, a snow-covered surface devoid of color and resplendent in white.

Earlier, Sharp explained to Kitty how Fisher could offer concise and deliberate theoretical descriptions and explanations of physics and the mechanics of flight. Help from Doug Geeting underscored the variety of lessons to be learned from others who were actively flying Alaska's glaciers. Doug emphasized using one's senses. He taught, as he wrote in his book *Mountain Flying*, "Your natural senses are your best friends in mountain country. Sight, sound and feel are your personal links to attitude flying. Let the instruments serve as a backup to your senses when you're in rugged terrain."

For glacier landings, Doug wrote, "Treat it much the same as you would a very soft-field landing. That is, overfly the surface first. Look for crevasses – notable lines that run perpendicular to the overall flow of the glacier. If you can see these lines, don't land near them. Rather, pick a spot between the lines. Check the slope of the glacier. Pick the longest, smoothest, flattest stretch you can find between the buried crevasses. Unless there is a strong tailwind, glacier landings are made upslope… Check the depth of the snow. A black plastic garbage bag with a couple of cans of Spam works best (if you get stuck, you can eat the contents.) Toss the bag out of the airplane from about 500 feet. If the bag bounces off the surface, the crust is iced over and a safe landing is possible, but don't expect the crust to be as hard as asphalt or concrete. Then, define a touchdown zone by dropping another bag in line with, and upslope from, the first. Flat light eliminates depth perception. So, the bags not only help define the touchdown zone but also provide a degree of depth perception."

He noted, "Glaciers have gradients. The steeper the gradient, the shorter the distance available for the aircraft to land and take off. Weight makes a difference, too, and Piper Cubs can operate with more agility than Cessna 180s and 185s. The Cessnas cannot turn as readily on steeper terrain. Some amazing nooks and crannies can be accessed in this manner," he continued. "Takeoffs are most exciting, as sometimes the terrain just drops out from beneath the airplane, you go negative and float up into your seat belt as you begin to free fall like that little elevator ride, down, down until the airspeed picks up, the wings generate lift, and you're flying. Reading the gradient of a glacier as you fly toward it is hard because there are usually no visual clues to give the pilot any depth perception. The first time I flew into the southeast fork with Don Sheldon, he dropped spruce boughs in over the landing area. When he came back in to land, he lined up on the boughs. When we touched down, the engine was developing full power, not a power setting usually associated with landing. The axiom that best explains the above is the 'point of no relative movement theory,' which is a military flying technique. The pilot sights on an object on the ground through the windshield and keeps it in a fixed place on the windshield throughout approach. If it moves below your mark, the aircraft will overshoot. If it moves above the mark, the aircraft is getting too low."

Kitty's Diary:

Jim and I had taken off in the Super Cub 7185 Bravo on wheel-skis from the dirt airstrip in the center of Talkeetna. The plane seemed to float up over the dense forest of hearty evergreens and ancient cottonwoods. We followed the braided rivers winding up toward the glacier source. Thick woods gradually thinned to straggly spruce trees, flowing into great rolling slopes of treeless tundra. As we gazed at the passing landscape it was a patchwork tapestry of greens and gold. Below, a black bear and her two cubs roamed over the land toward a sky-mirroring lake that was home to two trumpeter swans.

The land rises dramatically from 350 feet elevation in Talkeetna to 20,310 feet at McKinley's summit only 55 land miles away. The mountain's foothills grew larger before our eyes and Denali filled the windshield. The river we were following was getting more and more rugged. I could see where it originated; gushing out from beneath a mile-wide decaying terminal moraine. The milky water

Super Cub on Moose's
Tooth, Buckskin Glacier

Kitty & Super Cub,
Buckskin Glacier

bubbled from below and spouted like a geyser into a glacial lake, pouring into a rushing waterfall that carved downward into the rivers below. We flew over the gritty moraine onto the white expense of the glacier. The broad surface was a tangle of century old debris strewn with grit and rocks. Out of the corner of my eye I saw a strange, glowing, aquamarine color. Looking closer, I saw dozens of tiny turquoises anonymously dotting the white surface. They glowed like backlit gemstones, a spectacular effect caused by silt which is created when rocks below the surface of the ice are grinding from the movement of the glacier. The sunlight that reflects off this fine rock flower is absorbed in the glacier meltwater which gives the lakes their spectacular turquoise color.

Gaining altitude as we traveled above the sloping glacier, we flew through some gauzy, white clouds, clinging to the peaks rising from the sides of the glacier. Sharp pointed out our destination ahead, the Buckskin Glacier.

The nearby mountain, the Mooses Tooth, is a dramatic 10,335-foot rock peak on the east side of the Ruth Gorge.

My first instructional dual glacier landing on the Buckskin Glacier was magical. We circled high above the landing area and then swooped low to drag the skis through the snow without completely touching down. Jim did this at full power to test snow depth and to create good tracks for takeoff. Climbing and circling, he glanced around as part of his pre-landing check and he explained, "Almost full power is required with a fully loaded airplane, with flaps extended to achieve a zero-descent rate at 7,000 feet above sea level. You aren't coming down to the glacier; it is coming up to you."

Kitty, snowshoe packing runway, Buckskin Glacier

It felt as if we had landed on a huge goose-down pillow. We parked next to a beautiful icefall. Landing

Digging out for take-off, snowshoe runway, Buckskin Glacier

109

upslope, if the airplane's light, you don't have to turn around; but, it is best to face the airplane downhill, ready to get back into the tracks made by landing. We shut down, climbed out of the aircraft, and strapped on snowshoes. Slowly and carefully, we explored the "pillow," the wide and slow-moving river of snow and ice. I marveled at the enormity of the glacier with its sharp vertical walls and found it beyond belief to be in the midst of such a world. I was amazed at the magnitude, the solitude and the beauty. It was all so spectacular.

It was now time to grab the shovel, dig out the skis that had sunk into the snow, and stamp out the runway tracks with our snowshoes, in advance of takeoff. Jim demonstrated how to form a 200-foot runway by compressing the snow to the proper compaction required. The process took us a couple of hours. When the strip was packed, we performed a pre-flight check, hopped into the Cub, fastened the seatbelts and shoulder harnesses, and took off down the glacier. I was just taking it all in, and as we approached a cluster of crevasses, we lifted off, skimming above them and soaring into the air. I glanced down into the depths of the gaping slices that can never be taken for granted by a glacier pilot.

We flew low over the glacier for a full impact of the scene. I felt like I could almost dip my toes in the brilliantly-colored aqua ponds below. The glacier melted into rivers and the rivers wound their way back to Talkeetna. The glacier has a blue hue and, as you ascend the exquisite tarns (high glacier lakes) are a brilliant turquoise, accentuating the surroundings creating 'twelve shades of white.' It was like an Ansel Adams photograph with the gradations of light and shadows.

On June 10, 1977, I made my first SOLO glacier landing: five landings, in fact, and five takeoffs from the "Kahiltna International," an affectionate term for Kahiltna Base Camp.

Kitty solo landing Ruth Glacier Super Cub in center of photo

After many dual flights in the Super Cub with my instructor, Mike Fisher, my day was finally here. I arrived at the airport to check the weather and preflight the Cub. This time it was different. I would be alone.

First solo landing, Ruth Glacier

Fueling the plane, I made sure that the right tank had enough fuel for several landings on the glacier and return, plus 30 minutes of reserve. Using only the right tank assures that upon landing, the outboard wing will help maintain stabilization for the left turn on the glacier so that the inboard ski doesn't dig into the soft snow.

111

I checked that my charts and survival gear were on board for my Flight. Climbing into the Cub, I buckled into the three-harness seat belt, set the mixture, hit master and mags and then the starter. I clicked the mike and announced, "N7185 Bravo to file a flight plan to the mountain."

Revis answered from the fight service station in his familiar Texan drawl and wished me a good flight. I checked the controls, instruments and did my run up. All set to go.

On the roll for takeoff, the Cub came alive. Flying over the vast rivers and lakes I radioed "Sunflower" with a position report. I flew up over the Tokosha Mountains and climbed up toward One Shot Pass, where the green valleys and dark granite terrain turns to white.

One Shot is a narrow V-notch in the mountain at high altitude with potentially strong winds. Set up for approach is critical and to be crossed at a minimum safe altitude of 8,500 feet. The pass is ahead and I flew close to the wall, dipping a wing to shoot through the narrow gap at a 45-degree angle. I maintained a position to turn away from the ridge if a strong down draft should strike and I lose lift. It is a rush to clear the pass and fly over blinding white ice fields strewn with crevasses.

As I continued up the winding glacier, it amazed me to see the dark lateral moraines flowing down from the adjacent valleys joining the medial moraine. The rock debris with the snow and ice looked like a huge glacial highway. Spotting the aquamarine tarns, the small pools of melt-water reflecting a brilliant blue-green light looked like sapphires, made me smile. The Kahiltna Glacier is the longest glacier in Denali National Park. It is 45 miles long and 2 miles wide. The main channel runs due south between Mt. Foraker to the west and the twin-peaked mountain, Mt. Hunter, to the east and Mt. McKinley towering to the north. I made a 90-degree turn onto the tributary of the main Kahiltna Glacier, the southeast fork. I wanted to get a good look at the crevasses; base camp, with the colorful tents and the black trash bags tied to bamboo wands; trail markers, marking the landing site below. The area is about 2 miles long and one-quarter mile wide where several areas are evident with huge gaping crevasses.

After checking my landing checklist and insuring that the skis had been rotated in the down position, I flew the slot, setting up a constant rate of descent with power and attitude. The glacier filled the windshield, as a steep uphill grade. I picked a fixed spot ahead to focus on through the approach. In relation to the firewall, if it moves up I am too low and if it moves down I am too high. There is no go-around here. The final approach and landing need to be dead on. On descent, with a lack of depth perception because of flat lighting or bright white snow, I looked for side references on the rock and the climbers' wands marking the glacier. Because of the steep pitch, I touched down with close to full power so I could continue with momentum through the snow to make the left turn at the top of the landing area near base camp.

I cut the engine, climbed out of the Cub, and stood there on the glacier in the thin air, alone for a moment. All was quiet that day with an eerie stillness broken by far off rumbles of rock and ice slides from the towering mile-high granite walls above. Taking off downhill on the rutted snow, I pushed the stick forward to raise the tail and was finally airborne after the last bump. On my last takeoff, I flew toward Mt. Foraker as the glacier dropped away beneath me and made a left 90-degree turn down the Kahiltna, Talkeetna bound.

It was exciting to make my first solo glacier flight and, in fact, five takeoffs and landings that day. Today was my day and Frances and I cheered together on the glacier as I made my way into a select group. I'm an Alaskan glacier pilot.

The Kahiltna Base Camp was managed by a paid individual who camped for a matter of months onsite and coordinated communications between climbers, the air taxi offices in Talkeetna, and air taxi pilots via VHF radio. This extraordinary employment requires an individual or two who can take wintry outdoor camping to an exalted level. Temperatures might have been as warm as the sixties in Talkeetna, but might drop to 10°F above zero at altitude. The coldest recorded temperature on Denali was 95°F below zero and the first winter ascent party in 1967 experienced a wind chill of minus 148°F. Mountain climbing, mountain flying and mountain camping are not for the unprepared. Rare is an individual who would rough it at Kahiltna International Airport for the benefit, safety, and camaraderie of those challenging themselves to attain a personal climbing goal on the mountain.

Ed Homer would write later of the culture of the base camp in *The Hill.* "There was always some construction going on in the spring, including the annual building of base camp on the Kahiltna Glacier at Denali. It was our version of an Amish barn raising. The local air taxi operators throw in together on this one, on the theory that we all benefited from a well-stocked and well-struck base camp during climbing season."

Kitty joined the other air taxi pilots and climbers who made a temporary home at the base camp in making sure that food, shelter, and provisions were available. It meant an endless number of trips in which she and other air taxi operators would transport poles, canvas and supplies. She would meet countless international climbers in her visits to base camp. Many of the climbers didn't speak English. Language barriers, however, never stopped them from mutually enjoying a sunset or a salmon bake. Some brought gifts of flags from their countries. Japanese climbers presented her with ceremonial tea pottery, sake and carved wooden figures they had brought from Japan.

"The Germans and Austrians often brought Schnapps and I always hoped for chocolate from the French," she said. She even received the shirt off the back of an Italian climber named Romeo after she had admired his team's custom Cassin Ridge designed logo.

Japanese tea time

One day in Talkeetna, twenty Japanese climbers arrived and were waiting outside their tents for the rain to clear. As the rain got worse, Kitty invited them inside the Sheldon hangar for shelter. A shy, tiny Japanese woman was among them, one of the few Japanese women ever to attempt Denali.

Japanese windsock during tea time on glacier

Female climbers were unusual at that time. Kitty talked to her and the woman invited her to join in her tea ceremony. The Japanese lady taught Kitty Japanese card games and they became friends. Being the only women, Chiyoko got exclusive use of the hangar's bathroom while the rest of the climbers had to use the woods.

Kitty, Japanese gifts

There was a language barrier, but Kitty was used to communicating with the travelers regarding the most essential motivations. Sometimes there would be several different expedition crews from different countries sleeping on the hangar floor and speaking very little English. 'Good night' was expressed in a dozen different languages and everyone knew what it meant.

Unfortunately, tragedy struck. Chiyoko died on the mountain. One of the teams had been roped together and when one person fell into a crevasse, the others on the rope were pulled in with him.

Kitty's Diary:

Fired up the Super Cub with expedition load to the SE fork of the Kahiltna Glacier. Had coffee in radio tent with Jeff Lowe at base camp. Followed the C 185 over 10,000-foot ridge, over another glacier and ridge to the west fork of the Ruth. Landed by Japanese base camp with the fish flag flying and had ceremonial tea with Japanese expedition. Flew gear back to Talkeetna, beautiful turquoise glaciated lakes. Incredible flight with door dropped and window open while flying a few hundred feet over the crevasses. Love the thrill.

Kitty was one of the first women to make repeat takeoffs and landings to and from Alaskan glaciers, but she couldn't do it without radio operators on the ground. Her most memorable radio operator was Frances Randall, known as the Kahiltna Queen and guardian angel to the climbers on Denali. Randall was truly a lifeline between the climbers and the air service. She spent nine summers, starting in 1975, as 7,000-foot base camp radio operation operator on the Kahiltna Glacier assisting with the coordination on dozens of rescue operations. Her information radioed to those charged with delivering climbers to and from the mountain was invaluable, helping pilots assess proper timing for pickup and drop-off, which was essential information in any emergency. It was tough

Jeff Lowe, Brad Johnson, & Scott Johnson

117

for any individual to go up there and live on ice for several months. She wore her hair in pigtails secured with orange survey tape, black welder's goggles to prevent snow blindness, rubber knee boots, a down parka and an ancient straw hat that was slowly falling apart. She maintained close contact with those in Talkeetna who profited from her clever radio chatter and impromptu on-air violin concerts. Frances was fluent in several languages and her multilingual talents contributed to her ability to motivate waiting climbers to don snowshoes and vigorously pack the glacier's runway after snowstorms created powdery, deceptively deep conditions.

"It isn't your average nine-to-five job," Randall said.

She was also one of the first women to climb Denali, in 1964, and claimed several first ascents in Alaska. She held a degree in mathematics and played first violin section of the Fairbanks Symphony Orchestra.

The pilots greatly treasured Frances' service. To keep her happy and up on the mountain, local pilots kept up on delivery of a steady stream of libations, fresh fruit, and especially the killer Talkeetna Roadhouse cinnamon rolls. The climbing season, generally from April through July, put Randall at base camp for the length of that season every year. All the pilots stopped to visit with her, bringing food, carrying out laundry and returning it cleaned and folded.

Frances, originally hired by Cliff Hudson, was charged with reporting weather for the benefit of climbers as well as pilots. She tracked the constant procession of climbers as they arrived and departed. Kitty treasured Frances and everybody found her to be a sweetheart, but toward the end of the season, and understandably so, she was often at the brink of losing her mind.

One time, Jim Sharp and Kitty were met with a rare tirade. She was bellowing, "It's all white, white, white! Everything's so damn white! I'm sick of it!"

Sharp and climbing friends flew in later that night with a planeload filled with greenery. While Randall slept in her tent, they quietly unloaded the freshly cut branches of evergreen and cottonwood and artfully surrounded her snow-painted campsite. When she awoke and stepped out into the temporary 'forest' the next morning, she was overjoyed.

After her many months on the glacier, Randall radioed to Cliff Hudson to specifically request that Kitty pick her up to take her off the Kahiltna. Kitty, flying Cliff's Cub, decided to fly one of the most dramatic routes on return, flying low over the glacial valleys, and then with a sharp turn, vibrant colors filled the landscape. Randall was speechless as they made the turn. Kitty slowed, opened the window, and dropped the door to add to the experience. She made several low passes over the

Jim Sharp & Frances Randall,
Kahiltna National Forest

Jim Sharp, climbers, &
Frances Randall

119

Phil Eastley, Frances Randall,
& Doug "Dougal" McCarty

Talkeetna airstrip before landing so that many grateful folks were there to greet and thank Randall. She was so valuable to them for so many years. It was, though, her final flight from her beloved mountain. She soon learned that she had terminal cancer. A couple of years later, Randall phoned Kitty but never admitted to her failing health.

"It was a goodbye call. Frances told me that she never forgot that special flight we had and recalled the fireweed and bluebell bouquets that I surprised her with," remembered Kitty.

Frances Randall passed away in 1984 at 59.

Kitty, loaded Cub for
glacier flight

After the season in Alaska, Kitty flew home to her family's summer cottage to finish up her seaplane training under the watchful eye of Merle Patnode on the Chain of Lakes in Three Lakes, Wisconsin. Merle managed the Three Lakes Airport. He owned and flew many airplanes, including the Cessna 172 floatplane that Kitty flew.

During the summer season, Kitty was instructed by Mike Fisher on Christiansen Lake in Talkeetna; she piloted the float-equipped old Cessna 180 originally owned by Don Sheldon. Kitty savored the hours of water flying and profited from both Mike Fisher's instruction in the C180 floatplane and Merle's C172 floatplane with careful stewardship of the aircraft and the waters, receiving her seaplane rating September 8, 1977.

K2, C185 with two kayaks tied to the floats for transport

TKA log building, Denali, Dennis Cowals photo

CHAPTER EIGHT

Success

Cathedral Spires

Kitty headed back to Alaska in April with a layover in San Francisco. During the stop in the airport, she picked up a Sunday edition of the local *San Francisco Chronicle,* figuring it would be interesting reading during her long flight north.

Upon arriving in Anchorage, Kitty was greeted at the airport by Jim Sharp. He took her to the air taxi area, where the Super Cub on retractable skis was parked, and had her climb into the front seat. They flew direct to Denali and landed on the Little Switzerland Glacier. Kitty was pilot-in-command and elated to be flying once again to the glacier. From there they flew to Pirate Lake to spend the night in one of several cabins owned by the legendary Swiss-born mountain climber and guide, Ray Genet. Pirate was one of hundreds of remote lakes located near the terminal moraine of the vast Tokositna Glacier, which descends from the peak of Denali. The Cub on skis was perfect for landing on the still, frozen lake at the breathtaking location.

During the flight, Jim told her more about Ray Genet. In 1967, he participated in the first successful winter expedition to Mt. McKinley's summit led by Gregg Blomberg. Genet's accomplishments included the Seven Summits throughout the world: from Denali to Kilimanjaro, Elbrus, Vinson, Everest, Aconcagua and Australia's Kosciuszko. As Sharp put it, he was, "Inexhaustible."

Genet was known as "The Pirate" and was in demand because of his expertise in building log structures. He was also indispensable to the U.S. Air Force Search and Rescue teams based at Fairbanks. Just shy of six feet tall, lean, and laced with muscle, Genet stood out from the crowd. His chin was darkly bearded and his steely eyes flashed when he engaged others with his penetrating gaze. He bristled with a proud confident spirit. Genet would often send his expeditions in to the Kahiltna to start their assents a few days prior to his arrival. He would then, fully encumbered with supplies, power up to catch them at the Kahiltna Pass.

Sharp told Kitty that Genet's prowess was in assisting climbers toward summits, as well as rescuing the injured, lost, or those in peril. For so many mountain climbers, he made their mountain summit dreams come true, and by far filled the role of Talkeetna's most accomplished mountaineer.

As Kitty flew to the Little Switzerland area, Sharp told her the history of the reputable mountain that overwhelmingly filled their windshield. It grew dramatically larger as they approached, as if in the process of expanding, dwarfing the Super Cub as they neared. As Kitty flew on, she also absorbed the beauty below, following the glacier-fed rivers running from their sources far above on the mountain. They were lucky to have crystal clear weather. The entire Alaskan Range was bathed in pale light that reflected and enhanced the spectrum of its colors - evergreen forests rising to meet blue skies and frosted lightly with a dusting of white snow.

Sharp pointed out the landing site on the Pika Glacier and Kitty set up for approach. It was as exhilarating, as always, to slowly settle the plane onto the glacier. Shutting the engine down and climbing out, they stood in the amazing silence enhanced by the faint orchestra of sounds of water flowing and random rumblings from the mountains. She soaked in the experience and then they headed off toward Pirate Lake.

As they approached, Kitty banked the plane and Sharp pointed out seven cabins in the secluded woods surrounding the frozen lake. All were expertly built by the talented Genet and some of his climbing companions.

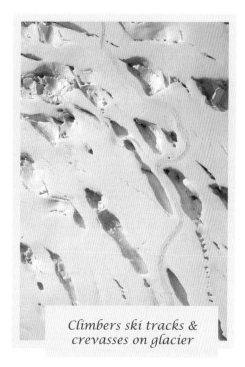

Climbers ski tracks & crevasses on glacier

The skis gently touched down on the frozen lake. At the cabin door stood a strong, attractive woman. It was Genet's partner, Kathy Sullivan. Kitty surprised her with that very morning's Sunday *San Francisco Chronicle*, which happened to be from Kathy's hometown and favorite newspaper. Kathy and Kitty hit it off right away as they prepared dinner. Sharp brought moose meat and wine, turning it into a feast. After dinner, Kitty and Kathy continued talking, discussing Genet's love for the area.

Kitty had met Genet several times prior. He was one of the first passengers she had flown, over churning river waters and cluttered sandbars, to locate wind-felled and river-beached logs for building his cabins.

The next morning, Kitty and Sharp found the ice on the lake to be much thinner than the evening before, but sufficient for the subsequent, uneventful takeoff. As they lifted over the trees at the end of the small lake, Sharp pointed out the Tokositnas, referring to them as "The Foothills." They gave incredible scale and beautiful depth to the domination of Denali as they turned away toward Talkeetna. Ahead and below them, winding rivers descended from their sources in the mountains. Off to their right was Swan Lake, a favorite calving area for moose. Often from the air, the calves could be spotted. They flew over large stands of aspen and willow, which decorated the banks of the ice-packed rivers, each carving their singular paths and seeming to challenge each other in a race from Denali to Talkeetna.

Kitty improvises, Cub dip stick turned moose meat skewer

Talkeetna presents the ultimate in bush flying: diversity in equipment and terrain. Each day was different, depending on the season, clientele, and Mother Nature. Pilots always packed their own airplanes. The center of gravity and weight distribution is critical to the aerodynamics of the aircraft's operation. Mountaineers would form an assembly line, passing backpacks and climbing equipment to the pilots, who would strategically place each item into the plane.

An average day during the height of the season, April through August, the pilots would often fly from around 6:00 a.m. until after midnight, weather permitting. Sometimes it would rain for days straight. But when the weather lifted and revealed the mountains, it was a race to get climbers and their supplies to their quests. There were flights for miners and trappers, along with fitting in the scenic trips for tourists awaiting their chances for once in a lifetime experiences.

Kitty & Cub loaded for glacier flight

First thing in the morning, Kitty would jump into the Cessna 185 on skis, fire it up, and fly to and from the glacier base camp. Later in the day, she'd switch into the Cessna 180 on floats and fly clients out to a remote lake. The day might cap off in the Super Cub, landing on a gravel river bar or dirt strip for a fisherman, game hunter, or a miner.

"Since seats weigh a bit and take up space, they were always removed. Climbers would sit on their backpacks instead, with the seat belts strapped over their laps, if they could find the belt," laughed Don Lee. "Sometimes it would be completely full. In fact, one pilot has the record of hauling eight Japanese in a 185."

Unloading climbing gear, Kahiltna Glacier

"Often, I would look behind me to see a jumble of arms and legs with gear packed to the ceiling as they craned with cameras clicking," Kitty recalled.

"You'll bulk out before you gross out," explained Mike Fisher. "Most of that stuff is fluffy sleeping bags, pads, and parkas."

Climbers were never fazed by having to hunker down for a flight atop their packs. This contrasted with some scenic customers who arrived in dress heels and light clothing.

"Once, I even retrofitted my own snowshoes so an older lady could stand on the glacier in her heeled pumps," Kitty smiled.

"Today, things are different," Fisher, said. "Now we do what are called standard passenger briefings. But in the old days you just stuffed everyone in and took off. Nowadays if an undercover safety examiner sees something he doesn't like, somebody loses their license."

Today, Talkeetna pilots have livestock scales to weigh passengers and equipment, but back then they would estimate their loads.

"Three big Germans could equal about five Japanese, and one moose could equal three or more men," Kitty laughed.

Kitty at controls, C185, Dennis Cowals photo

Kitty recalled one of her earliest flights to Denali in the Super Cub, a harrowing experience to a pilot new to the terrain. Flying out of the Ruth Gorge, following Jim Sharp holding back the faster C185, Kitty suddenly became enveloped in a filmy, low-lying, white cloud that obscured her route. Unnerved, she keyed the mike and radioed to Sharp to report her scary situation, well aware of the consequences of even a minor mistake.

He responded urgently, "Hug that rock wall to your right - your three o'clock position."

She double-clicked in quick response and tried to stay calm as she guided the plane closer to her only reference, the sheer granite wall. For several minutes in severe visibility, Kitty wondered if she would fly into the clear. Sharp constantly reported his positions as he led her out of the gorge.

Mike Fisher later commented on Sharp's ability to slowly fly the Cessna, saying, "It takes work to steady a Cessna at low speeds."

On a beautiful Sunday morning without a cloud in the sky, Kitty fired up the Super Cub with expedition loads to take to the southeast fork of the Kahiltna Glacier. She visited on the glacier with some of the climbers while Sharp landed in the C185 with the rest of the gear. Wanting to do recon on some of the other climbers, they both took off and Kitty followed the C185 over the 10,000-foot ridge onto another glacier, another ridge to the west fork of the Ruth Glacier where they spotted the Japanese with their colorful fish kites flying high. They both landed their airplanes and made it over to camp and enjoyed teatime with the Japanese. Kitty loaded some gear and noted the flight back was spectacular over the beautiful, turquoise glaciated lakes with the window open while flying a few hundred feet over the crevasses down through the gorge. Later that night back in Talkeetna, another Japanese expedition invited Sharp, Kitty, and Joe "Mr. Joe" Troise to the Rainbow Lodge for steak and whiskey to celebrate their climb.

On June 6, a South African expedition arrived in town, which included the first South African woman to join their team. After waiting out many days of bad weather in the Buckminster Fuller Geodesic Dome, they finally received good news: a short break in the weather.

South African Expedition

Sharp flew the climbers and supplies to the southeast fork of the Kahiltna Glacier in the Cessna 185.

For the last run to the mountain, Kitty crammed into the pilot seat in the Super Cub, along with all the necessary remaining gear packed around her, and flew up to the mountain hoping to beat the weather. Nearing the entrance to One Shot Pass, she pushed for more altitude. The usual downdrafts were tugging at the airplane while approaching the knife-edge crossing as she flew over the ridge, then continued on to the Kahiltna Glacier base camp.

The conditions upon landing were close to whiteout, but wands in the snow gave definition to the base camp landing area. Five minutes later, a snowstorm engulfed them. Kitty unloaded the Cub, grabbed her sleeping bag, and prepared to spend time snowed in on the glacier.

The South African expedition leader had come back to base camp from ferrying the first load of supplies up the glacier and was so happy to receive the necessary last load. He then sledded back up the glacier to meet his team members, yet it didn't look like Kitty would be able to takeoff any time soon. Luck was with her, however, as her friends Michael Covington and Fred Phinney appeared in the whiteout.

After descending from the summit of Denali, more friends appeared. Galen Rowell, photojournalist, and Ned Gillette, former Olympic cross-country skier, had flown in earlier to attempt a world-record 48-hour ascent and were waiting for the storm to subside.

All of them ended up in the radio tent with Frances talking and drinking steaming cups of hot Tang. They kept their ears perked for any radio chatter about the weather forecast and climbers up high.

For the next 30 hours, Kitty ventured out into the storm to rope off the accumulating snow on the plane's wings. "It just kept coming down," she said. Every couple of hours she and another climber carefully shoved off the wet, heavy, goose-down flakes.

Kitty caught a few winks in a two-man tent, napping in between the sleeping bags of Covington and Phinney, who kept her awake while laughing with their raucous jokes and malodorous mountaineering scents.

To prepare for the flight tests for commercial pilots within the shadows of Denali, Kitty immersed herself into training with Mike Fisher. In addition to flying the ski-equipped aircraft, she logged dual training with Fisher to acquire timing and the control input necessary to perform precise chandelles, figure eights, Dutch Rolls, and other coordination exercises. She coupled flight familiarization and an intense study of the Alaskan wilds with simulated emergencies, including the loss of electrical and vacuum systems, performing steep turns and steep gliding spirals, and practicing engine-out procedures.

Recognizing her growing strengths, Mike Fisher signed her off for the commercial check ride, which she successfully completed with Fred Fechner, the Anchorage General Aviation District Office (GADO) examiner. No longer would she be restricted to carrying passengers within 50 nautical miles of her base. And, while flying as a commercial pilot, she could accept payment for her work. She logged "Partial panel hood work, unusual attitude recoveries, 720-degree steep turns, steep gliding spirals, accelerated stalls, takeoff, departure, and approach to landing stalls, and demonstrated proficiency at challenges such as reacting to in-flight fire, power loss, cross-wind takeoff and landings, and wheel landings." Fisher was thorough and extremely precise. Her learning curve broadened and that enhanced her confidence.

Later, confirming that Mike Fisher was pleased with her progress and comfortable with her achievements, he took it upon himself as Chief of Flight Training Operations to write a letter on Kitty's behalf to the representative of the GADO. He sought permission to add her as a pilot to the Talkeetna Air Taxi Part 135 Certificate. It was a stunning endorsement of her piloting skills and the contributions she could bring to the air service.

Mike Fisher wrote in his first humorous draft:

Mike Fisher & Kitty,
Commercial rating briefing

Mr. Fred Fechner:

Thank you for your attention to our check-ride needs on June 20th. We try hard to maintain high standards and are pleased with recognition for our efforts. We would like to add Catherine Ann Banner to our Part 135 Certificate as a pilot. It is our belief that she can do a very good job for us within the limitations of her certificate. On reviewing the Federal Aviation Regulations, FARS, Parts 61 and 135, we find that she complies with 61.123, 61.125 (A), 61.127 (A), 61.129 (A and B), 135.33, and 135.35, as well as the pilot requirements of the Talkeetna Air Taxi Part 135 Approved Operations Specifications.

We realize it is a bit unorthodox to employ a pilot with a limited Commercial Certificate in Air Taxi Work. However, we have many flights that can be accomplished without going beyond a 50-mile radius or flying at night. Naturally, we would not be sending her out with hazardous materials (unless one calls Ray Genet a hazardous material) or in poor weather until she acquires more experience and an instrument rating. Please give some consideration to helping us include Ms. Banner in our Part 135 Certificate with the understanding that she will not be required to exceed the limitations stated on her commercial pilot certificate.

Thank you very much,

Michael J. Fisher,
Chief of Flight Training Operations

On June 20, 1978, Kitty passed her Commercial check ride and celebrated with a big cookout in the front yard at the Talkeetna Air Taxi log building. The group was a who's who of well-known, accomplished mountain climbers, including Yvon Chouinard, rock climber, environmentalist, and founder of Patagonia outdoor clothing from California; Henry Barber, a well-known rock climber from Boston; and Rudi Hamberger, Swiss nature photographer and accomplished climber. They had just arrived off the mountain after being flown in weeks earlier. Sharp had flown them onto a tight, flat, side glacier by Mt. Dickey off the Ruth Glacier. After his takeoff, Kitty followed and landed with a visual of his tracks to deliver their gear.

Commercial rating congrats

Joining the celebration were friends and climbers in town: Michael Covington from Colorado, founder of Fantasy Ridge Guiding Service, renowned climber, and accomplished musician; Fred Phinney, rock climber from New Hampshire; Roberta Sheldon and her kids, Holly, Kate, and Robert; along with Mike, Suzanne, and Mary Murphy.

Yvon Chouinard &
Rudi Hamberger, 1978

On July 18, Kitty passed her Commercial Part 135 check ride with an FAA examiner and then her Part 135 check rides in the Cessna 185 wheel/skis, Super Cub (PA18) wheel/skis, and Cessna 180 seaplane in Talkeetna. Now she had all her certificates to fly commercial flights to glaciers, lakes and into the backcountry. She was no longer a *"pilota bandida."*

New climbers in town weren't necessarily accustomed to flying with a woman. Kitty drew more than her share of raised eyebrows when she would grab climbers' duffle bags and supplies from the ramp and hoist them up into the aircraft. She then methodically loaded them into the cabin, careful to avoid interference with operation of controls, rudder cables, and door handles. Heavier items would be forward to keep the center of gravity of the plane balanced for safe flight. Once the customers were in, she would fill the spaces around them with the lighter items. No questions were asked until she climbed into her seat at the controls and turned to ask with her bright smile, "Is everyone good to go?" At that point, occasionally, she heard a concerned voice from a passenger, "Where's the pilot?"

Rather than explaining, she gave a safety briefing and turned to the business of firing up the throaty Cessna. Ready to taxi, she looked back at her passengers, who were often belted in atop their firmly stuffed backpacks. Once airborne, her passengers became more aware of their special surroundings in the Alaska wilderness. Kitty often gave a brief overview, and by the time they landed on the glacier, she had made new friends. Some of them stayed in touch over the years with Christmas cards and postcards of their climbs around the world.

June was a busy month for Kitty. She was sitting at her desk when out of the blue, a call came in from the Yukon, "Arriving in Anchorage at 6:30 p.m. Mary "Murf" Murphy, a lifelong friend and cousin from Chicago, was coming to visit.

Soon after, a rescue call came over the radio. A client of Genet's wanted a rescue at 14,300 feet on the glacier. Jim Sharp flew a risky mission on oxygen to evacuate the injured climber, Dr. Fleet Ratliff, high up on the glacier in the Super Cub. Genet was there to help facilitate the pick-up. They landed back in Talkeetna, and after refueling, Kitty flew Ratliff to Anchorage and picked up Mary when her flight arrived. She stayed in Talkeetna and helped out at TAT. Mary had a great sense of humor and she could always get Kitty to laugh. They often found themselves dancing to a blue grass band or doing the Irish jig until the music stopped.

Kitty had a couple of PA-18 Cub runs to the southeast fork of the Kahiltna. She flew to base camp and picked up Cindy, a temporary base camp operator who had been there for many weeks. With a full load, Kitty took off the glacier for a flight through Second Shot Pass, cruising low over crevasses and green glacial valleys. But then, en route back to Talkeetna, Kitty recycled the skis to wheels to find there was a failure in the hydraulic retractable wheel ski system. The system wasn't holding correct fluid level for pressure so there was a small hand-held pump-can on board to fill the reservoir. As Kitty squeezed the pump, fluid sprayed onto her and the floor. She looked out to see if both skis had retracted and saw that only one ski was

up. She was forced to land on one wheel, keeping the ski off as long as possible to save it from damage on touchdown. Not knowing the few squeezes of the can had raised the ski just enough to expose the bottom of the wheel, Kitty put the Cub down on the threshold without event. However, the ski was dragging enough that Kitty and Cindy got out and walked to the air taxi building.

The annual Moose Drop Festival began with a parade only Talkeetna could put on. Old cars, trucks, and homemade vehicles loaded with wildly dressed occupants made the procession distinctly memorable.

14,300' base camp

Sharp & Genet, rescue at 14,300'

With a short break in the flying action, Kitty celebrated along with the rest of the town. Some say the festival is traced back to 1972 when a few of the local lads were living it up in the Fairview Inn and thinking of ways to attract tourists to Talkeetna. Other documentation says that the Talkeetna Historical Society invented the infamous Moose Toss game. They decided to turn their attention to a festival honoring the Alaska moose, or more specifically, its poop. They collected moose droppings from the forest, baked them in an oven, and sprayed them with varnish. The first game was the "moose nugget-tossing contest" that involved tossing the varnished droppings onto a board with numbers. The numbers were tallied up at the end of the game and the person with the highest total was the winner and received a prize. The Historical Society ran the Moose Drop Festival as a fundraising event for 37 years.

After the parade, games, and bake sale, Doug, Jim, Roberta, Kitty, and two other pilots flew six airplanes over town. They made three low passes over town in tight formation. The town of Talkeetna danced in the street until late into the night.

Doug, Mary, & Ken,
tough day fishing, Clear Creek

On July 20, a call came in about a crash in the Cashe and Bird Creek area that was believed to have two fatalities. Sharp responded to the SOS. and asked Don Lee to come along. Kitty tossed in a sleeping bag at the last moment. It proved to be essential emergency survival gear. The two men departed for the area not knowing if the accident had occurred in Bird Creek or Cashe Creek. They took off without knowing a rescue helicopter was headed for the rocky, tree-lined canyons in search of the accident. That pilot turned back because of poor visibility and heavy winds in the target area. Sharp and Lee were headed for trouble.

Later, Sharp wrote of the crash in his memoir, *Glacier Driving*: "The airplane hit hard on one wing and cartwheeled up the canyon. Our emergency gear flew out the right side. The landing gear came up through the floor and broke my leg; there was a cloud of dust, flying Plexiglas, rapid deceleration, the feeling of being flung around hard against the sides of the cockpit. The shoulder harness and seat belt stretched and I hit the instrument panel. My passenger, Don Lee, appeared out in the rain. I quickly told him about the emergency gear and he went down a little draw and retrieved it. Lee had been living in the bush, he was 23 years old, he was strong, and he was probably in shock. He returned with the sleeping bags, helped get me out of the wreck and set up camp for us under the wing. Didn't know it at the time, but I had five compressed vertebrae, a fractured ankle and broken ribs, among other injuries."

Sharp and Lee had accidentally made the exact mistake that the other downed pilot and passenger made. Flying too low and slow and looking at the crash site, they had been sucked into an accelerated stall that resulted in a horrific crash.

"We sat under the wing for about six hours," Lee remembered. "I'd say, 'Oh, I think I broke my legs.' Jimmy would say, 'Oh, I think my back's broken.' And I'd say, 'Oh, I think my arm's broken' . . . it went on until the Sea Stallion rescue chopper appeared out of the clouds," said Lee. "They had a special litter that picked you and the dirt you were sitting on up and whisked you away." Lee recalled.

Kitty got the call at 6:30 the next morning from Revis at the Talkeetna Flight Service Station about the crash in Bird Creek. Kitty and Mike Fisher flew the C185 down to Anchorage to go to Providence Hospital to visit Sharp and Lee, who were in pretty bad shape. Sharp needed surgery and was in ICU for a while in a body cast and Lee remained in the hospital as well, also in a body cast until the middle of August. She visited them often and brought them back to Talkeetna in a station wagon with an air mattress in the back.

Kitty knew that Lee was back out at the camper in the woods with his siblings after returning from the hospital in Anchorage. She decided to make something special for them. Mike Fisher's partner, Suzanne, gave her some tall stalks of rhubarb she had harvested from her garden and fresh rhubarb pie sounded delicious. Armed with a recipe, Kitty went to work rolling the dough and preparing chunks of the sweetened red vegetable that, when hot and syrupy, oozed up through tiny slits in the top crust that looked like lipstick kisses. While the pies were just out of the oven, she hopped into the pickup and headed into the woods, ignoring that spring rains had soaked the area and the already rough going was riddled with deep puddles.

Not quite sure where to find Lee and his siblings in the woods, Kitty drove in the direction she had been told. She came to a deep waterhole in the dirt road and pushed on a bit quickly hoping to not sink, but water splashed up onto the engine and killed it. Kitty tried to start it, but to no avail - at least until the distributor dried out. After waiting some time, she turned the key, and with a growl, it coughed and started. She was heading deeper into the woods. Then, amidst boughs and stringy willows, the camp appeared, shaded and protected by its overgrown habitat.

She parked and climbed out of the truck with the pies, which were still warm. They ran out with excited smiles to greet her and wasted no time to talk and eagerly reached for the pies, ran back inside and devoured them. She felt like an elf in the forest delivering a treat, and was so happy that she had found them.

WILD MOUNTAIN by
Shannon Cartwright

Jody Lee's thank you
for pies and artwork

The accident in July that injured and hospitalized Sharp and Don brought Kitty to a new challenge.

Sharp and Steve Hanson designed and had agreed with Larry Rivers and Ralph Wing to build a spacious, two-story log building that would be the Talkeetna Air Taxi base of operations. While Sharp was the owner of the new building, his injuries led to prolonged absences. This change put an additional load on Kitty's responsibilities and flight schedule.

She remembered, "In addition to being the office manager and pilot of the busy air taxi service, I became more involved in the completion of the log building."

Kitty's Diary:

August 7th. Kathy was pregnant with her and Genet's first child. At 4:30 a.m., I was wakened with a call from Dorothy at the grocery store. She was relaying a radio-patch message through the Bush Pipeline, as the only radio in the village was at Dorothy's home store.

A few days earlier, I had flown to Pirate Lake to check on Kathy and I'd found her alone, but happy and ready, if necessary, to deliver the baby on her own. I told her Genet should be coming off the mountain soon to be with her and, not wanting to leave the sanctuary of Pirate Lake, Kathy insisted on staying, so I gave her a box of fresh vegetables from our friend, Ed Craver's, garden. Feeling her rooting instincts and maternal nesting, she had started a garden of her own from seed and, not having seen freshly picked radishes and thinking they were bulbs, she said, 'Goodbye,' waved briefly, and went off to plant the already ripened vegetables in her patch, hoping that the black and brown bears didn't get to them before they could take root.

When I saw Genet just off the mountain on the evening of the 5th at the Ol' Fairview Bar with his French client, I reminded him that Kathy was due any moment and in need of someone with her. He assured me he was waiting for a doctor friend from Seattle who would arrive any day, at which time they would fly directly to the lake. Genet, feeling nervous, had Cliff Hudson fly him and the Frenchman in the next morning, the 6th.

The radio patch to Dorothy was Genet requesting that I fly in for an immediate pick-up. I headed down the gravel road in the old pickup truck to the Cessna 180 on

Floatplane pick up for bear skin

Christiansen Lake. I calculated and fueled from the 55-gallon barrel of avgas (aviation fuel). It seemed to take forever to pump the excess water out of the EDO floats due to leaky rivets and, as I continued to pump, I thought of the flight ahead.

As I taxied down the lake, there was not a whisper of a wind, which would make takeoff difficult when the craft was fully loaded. But, that situation was already one with which I was familiar due to Genet's often overloaded flights to and from the mountain during his expeditions.

I took off and headed north to Pirate Lake, which ran toward the south just off the Tokositna River and two miles south of the terminal moraine of the Ruth Glacier. Weather was low. I set up for a touchdown on the lake over the rocks on the south end and short of the swamp on the north end, sweeping into a right angle turn to taxi to the dock and avoid any large rocks under the water.

It was a relief to see Genet, the Frenchman, and Kathy, smiling in her big sweatshirt. I was convinced she was primed to deliver her baby and ready to depart Pirate Lake. I was so happy Genet heeded my warning and obviously came in to be with Kathy.

I quickly assessed the mounds of supplies needing to be loaded into the aircraft strategically and quickly before the floats filled up with water due to the extra weight. In true Alaskan fashion, foul weather was moving in from the north and visibility was already dropping in the direction of our departure path, predicated upon the shortness of the lake and rocks in the water.

Unfortunately, the surface of the lake was calm before the storm, which might impede our departure. As I climbed to the back of the aircraft, Genet tossed a bag for me to stow out of the way of controls or any strategic cables. He then tossed a wicker basket filled with linens. I caught it, thinking it was merely laundry, and started to swing it into the back recess of the plane, only to hear his loud guffaw of laughter and to glance up to see a huge grin light his face. I looked more closely at the fabrics in the basket and, hearing a whimper from underneath the folds, I unwrapped the covering to reveal a twenty-hour-old baby.

My surprised reaction excited Genet and he, Kathy, and I shared a valuable moment of wonder. I realized how very precious was this cargo and how timely his birth. Luckily, Genet and the Frenchman had found Kathy in labor in the cabin. Neither man had delivered a baby before, but they wisely hammered pitons into the log bed for Kathy to grip and to push against. They told me later that, after a few hours of labor, a healthy, beautiful baby boy was born named Taras Genet.

I realized that a storm was rushing preparations for takeoff and faced the task of getting my three passengers, baby, and gear into the floatplane, off the lake, and safely back to Talkeetna. I quickly climbed in, started the engine, and taxied to position the aircraft for takeoff. The lake was as calm as glass creating suction, hindering the ability to get the plane off the water. By taxing on the step, I created a wave action to break the suction. It was not quite enough. With the chopped-up water, we made another attempt and succeeded in passing the cutoff point along the shoreline with enough speed to lift off and climb out. Right then that little Taras gave out his baby bellow, his Alaskan cry to Denali and its range, his confirmation of his arrival.

Turning away from the impending storm, we headed south along the Tokositna River toward Talkeetna, where the rivers rejoined. Kathy and Taras were healthy and strong and Genet was rejuvenated after a grueling expedition he had just successfully completed on 'The Great One.' We all realized that with the countless adventures we shared together in Alaska, there had never been a more blessed moment than the birth of this child. I realized that not only did I love my flying work in Alaska, but how important my

*Kitty, Private lake floatplane pick up,
Kathy & Taras Genet newborn*

job was to others who live in the bush and depend upon me and others like me - kindred spirits shared by adventurers and linked by our needs.

As we banked to descend and land in Talkeetna, we celebrated Taras' arrival anew by sharing the sky with a pair of Trumpeter Swans in takeoff for their morning flight. At the moment, we had no doubt Taras would grow to be a mountain climber.

Two weeks after his birth, I flew a load of supplies to Stephan Lake, unloading the cache and carrying some of it inside the beautiful lodge. I was invited in for a cup of coffee, and when I entered, a very large German hunter in traditional German garb was seated at the log table. I heard that Genet and Kathy were in the area, so I asked the hunter whether he had seen them.

His answer, delivered in a broken Deutsch-English accent that went along with his vigorous nod of his head, was, "Ja! Kati vas here, baby in buckskin on front, leg of moose meat strapped on back, .45 pistols packed on side. Got in canoe, paddled cross lake, hiked to half-way hut" (a log cabin provided for hunters to stay when bringing their sheep down from the high country).

Hoping to catch sight of Kathy, I said my goodbyes. I then fired-up the C180 green and white floatplane 74X and took off to fly over the autumn tundra and up to the cabin to check on Kathy and Taras. After circling the cabin three times, Kathy recognized the friendly floatplane and came out with Taras in her arms to wave happily. Seeing they were all right, I waved my wings and headed back to Talkeetna.

Ray Genet did not survive a climb on Mt. Everest. It was confirmed that Genet died on October 2, 1979, while descending. He succumbed to hypothermia while Kathy, pregnant with Adrian, and Taras, a toddler, were at an Everest base camp. It was a shock to the town of Talkeetna. His presence was larger than life and would be missed by the climbing community throughout the world. Genet's legacy was honored when his son, Taras Genet, became the youngest mountaineer to reach the summit of Denali on June 25, 1991, at the age of 12.

Kitty's Diary:

My birthday started early with a beautiful flight with Murf in Doug's Taylorcraft. We flew the river and spotted several eagles that were out for an early morning flight as well. After our flight, Suzanne and Mike came over for breakfast and coffee at the TAT log building. That evening, we had a fun Mexican birthday dinner feast, cake and all, with Kimball, Roberta, Jim Shaff, Murf and Doug. Later in the evening, at the Fairview bar, we had shots of tequila and then went over to the park to see the Dr. Ogstad Old Fashion Traveling Medicine Show from Fairbanks. They had their tent set up for the show. Roberta volunteered me to go on stage, drink the elixir and kiss the frog that later turns into a prince, clad in tennis sweater, racket and all.

Three days later, an overbooked Cliff Hudson asked me to pick up 'two and a moose' at a lodge on Schulan Lake, a remote lake close to the Yetna River. I was given a heading to the west. I flew N2774X to what I thought was the lake and cabin. Not completely sure, I landed. I saw a cabin and an old-timer came out onto the bank.

I yelled out, asking him, "Is this Schulan Lake?"

He replied, "It's that-a-way," pointing to the west.

I thanked him and flew away.

I located the lake and after landing, I taxied up toward the lodge. There ahead, I could see about 15 huge, burly hunters covered in blood from butchering their moose kills sitting on the hill along the bank. Shutting down the engine, I opened the door and stood on the float. They were all anxious and waiting for a flight out to Anchorage before the weather closed in.

Kitty, N2774X floatplane fuel check, Dennis Cowals photo

*Cliff Hudson, moose antlers secured,
Super Cub on gravel bar*

So, I looked at these guys staring at me and I kind of dropped my octaves and said, "I'm here for two and a moose for Hudson."

The men were surprised at seeing a female pilot. I assumed that some of these guys had been drinking and there they were, sitting with their rifles. This one guy, the biggest, burliest, and toughest-looking guy, stood up in front of the whole lot and shouted: "Hey, lady, aren't you the one who kissed the frog?"

The group broke out in laughter as many of them had been in Talkeetna and had seen the Dr. Ogstad Troupe Traveling Show days before. It broke the ice right there.

Bush and glacier flying held myriad of challenges. Carrying hunters, their equipment, and their bounty obviously presented increased workloads. In taking rifles aboard aircraft, for example, they had to be emptied of ammunition and placed aboard by the pilot so they did not interfere with the controls of the aircraft. Tents, sleeping bags, food, and clothing had to be strategically placed in concern for weight, balance, and inevitably, in loading the carcass, blood would splatter on the pilot and throughout the craft.

Mike Fisher taught me his rule: to assure no meat was wasted. Always fly the moose meat out first with one of the passengers to help unload and then return to pick up the remaining passenger and gear. Experience taught me that some hunters would leave the meat rather than pay for the second flight out. Hunters couldn't refuse paying for the final flight, if it was for personal evacuation.

Out of the group, the 'two and a moose' clients of Cliff Hudson's that I had come to pick up stepped forward with their gear and their moose. As I was loading the floatplane I asked if their rifles were empty, they assured me they were but upon my inspection, they weren't. They emptied the guns and I placed them in the plane. While loading the aircraft, I said that I would take one guy and the moose meat out on the first trip. They argued with me with urgency and insisted I take all the moose meat, all their gear, and both of them. Instead of arguing, knowing they would have to pay for the extra tach time, I told them that we would be overloaded but complied to prove the point that the airplane was too heavy. I pumped out the floats, loaded the bloody moose meat, loaded their gear and had them climb into the cramped cabin.

I taxied out and asked them to look down to check the floats, and to their surprise, they answered, "The floats are mostly submerged and I think we're sinking!"

Point proven, we taxied back and unloaded one of the guys, his gear and his rifle, keeping the meat aboard. I knew they would pay for the second trip back to pick up the second guy and his gear!

The busy season was closing and Kitty welcomed late autumn. The time came to take the C180 floatplane down to Lake Hood and help the mechanic, Roger Borer, convert from floats to wheels. Then it came time to fly down to the lower 48. Sharp and Kitty left Talkeetna in the fully loaded C185. It was two hours to Northway, Alaska, and another two hours to Whitehorse, Yukon Territory, Canada. The last hour, as darkness fell, they watched for car headlights on the Al-Can Highway in light turbulence under a ceiling of cloud at 6,000 feet.

Floats to wheels with Roger Borer, Lake Hood

The next morning's flight took them to Watson Lake. Kitty and Sharp took a break and had lunch sitting on the airplane's tires. While taxing for takeoff, there was a great surprise. Kimball Forrest just landed in his newly purchased Cessna 180, 92CP. He heard Kitty on the radio. They then took off together and had a beautiful flight in formation through spectacular terrain. They put down in McKenzie, British Columbia, to get some food and to spend the night.

Flying formation again the next morning, they headed to Bellingham, Washington. It was a spectacular flight through the British Columbia mountains and Kitty landed at the Bellingham International Airport through a brush fire haze. After spending the night and talking with Kimball's father, they all took off in formation, once again flying the C185 and C180 over the Cascade Mountain Range and passing Mt. Baker, Mt. Rainier, Mt. St. Helens and Mt. Hood. They flew in and out of each other's wakes and then waved wings to say goodbye. Kimball headed east to Denver and Kitty and Sharp south to the Trout Lake Oregon Tea Farm, landing on the grass strip just south of Mt. Adams.

Cathedral Spires glacier landing tracks

Luau, Circle Hot Springs, Houston Oil and Minerals, Kimball's C180

CHAPTER NINE

Inspiration

Kitty headed for Colorado's Jefferson County Airport in Broomfield to prepare for her instrument rating. She purposely chose Hoffman Pilot Center to work with its president, Harry LaFarge, an exceptional airman honored as a "Rocky Mountain Region and Colorado District Flight Instructor of the Year." She had previously worked with LaFarge to complete her ground training and fly phase checks.

"The Art of Giving encompasses many areas. It is an outgoing, overflowing way of life. "We give of ourselves when we give the gift of Inspiration..."

—Peterson

While she was pursuing the additional ratings in the Boulder area, she and Kimball Forrest had time to rekindle their friendship. He worked as a geologist with Houston Oil and Minerals in Denver (HOM). Kimball had completed his instrument rating and he helped her work toward her written and flight tests. Kitty took her FAA instrument written while Kimball was taking his instructor exam just one table over.

WINGS OF HER DREAMS

Kitty's diary noted the date: "FINISH—easy exam, lunch in Denver, margaritas and dancin' on Colfax."

A couple of days later, they decided to take an "under the hood" trip in the Cessna 180 *92CP*, "Charlie Pop." Heading south, she practiced instrument flying to Amarillo, Texas. They had dinner followed by some country swing at the local country bar. The next day, they took off, circled the Cadillac Ranch and then flew through the box canyon south of Amarillo just off the deck – all for fun.

On April 24, 1979, Kitty passed her instrument check ride.

Her reconnection with Kimball was serendipitous. Handsome, energetic, and confident, he was also an accomplished pilot with many logged flight hours and valuable experience and expertise in airplanes. Later in life, as he jokingly says, he turned to the dark side: helicopters. He had hundreds of skydives and took his turn at the controls of the skydiving aircraft. Kimball is remembered at his high school for having parachuted onto the ball field for his graduation ceremony.

Kitty had learned a great deal flying with Talkeetna Air Taxi, but now she was ready to move forward. Kimball told her that the company he worked for, Houston Oil and Minerals, was going to do mineral exploration in Alaska. While it was based out of an office in Denver, Colorado, it included a satellite office in Anchorage. He went on to tell her they had plans for exploration work, and while she was in Colorado, he introduced her to the project manager at the Denver office who was responsible for the management of exploration in Alaska. While still a good friend with Sharp, who had given her many opportunities, complications arose after the summer of 1978 with the air taxi and his FAA Medical. Kitty decided to make a change. She left Talkeetna Air Taxi for HOM. Everything moved quickly after that. She was hired as a job expediter and started on the first of May in Denver. She flew to Alaska to set up the Anchorage Office for HOM. The position entailed expediting shipments to and from the geologists, geomorphologists, engineers and drillers for geological exploration in Alaska. At the same time, Kimball worked on the North Slope as a geologist involved in mineral exploration. Kitty saw the HOM job as a chance to save some of her salary toward what was now her bigger dream, to return to Talkeetna in the future and fly the area once again as the owner of her own air taxi service.

Covering five camps throughout Alaska and two in British Columbia, she needed help with base operations and hired Mary Murphy for the position. The new position came not only with aerial experiences, but new driving experiences. One job involved delivering geophysical gear to Canada. The trip began with driving to Whitehorse on the Al-Can Highway through the rain and mud, a challenging road even when dry.

Murf, Circle Hot Springs

En route, Kitty got a flat tire at 1:00 a.m. She was covered in mud in her attempt to fix the problem, before two cars luckily stopped to help. Back on the road by 3:00 a.m., she drove from Whitehorse to Watson Lake, down the Cassiar Highway, which was mostly dirt, and past Telegraph Creek and Stikine River.

She arrived at Mezziadin Lake Lodge, where she found the proprietor to be drunk. Covered with mud and exhausted, she slept with all her clothes on in a cold room with mosquito wall décor. She woke the next morning, met with the geologist to unload the geophysical gear and headed back to Watson Lake.

That day on the road, she came upon a car with several native guys who had a rifle pointed at a Fish and Wildlife officer. Kitty slowed, hoping that the officer might possibly be able to latch on and escape from the situation, but with no luck. She arrived at Watson Lake at midnight because the road was closed due to a washed-out bridge. She rented a cabin at a lodge and reported the incident that she had seen on the road. The next morning, she endured an 18-hour marathon drive back to Fairbanks and on to the Livengood Mine to meet her friend, Tom Lamal "Bullet," for 4th of July festivities.

With the beautiful midnight sun, she could see Denali in the clear. Days later, another job involved flying in the right seat with Buddy Woods in the Otter delivering equipment to a camp in the Port Alsworth area through Lake Clark Pass. At 2,500 feet elevation, the pass is more than 75 miles long and just wide enough for two planes to pass in opposite directions. Spectacular waterfalls cut their way through knife-edge crevasses. Many airplanes have gone down in the pass in bad weather.

One of the advantages to the job was to get flight time when contracting the different air charter services to deliver camp supplies throughout the state. The job also had another important advantage: it allowed Kitty and Kimball to make plans for their future business.

Kitty's Diary:

Tony Martin and I met while relocating a camp as part of my role with Houston Oil and Minerals. I had contracted a Skyvan out of Anchorage, which turned out to be a boxy-shaped combination of a cargo aircraft and airliner - an ungainly but sturdy twin-engine craft piloted by a crusty old 'Alaskan been-all-over-the-world sort of guy,' Bob Clark. He smoked big cigars while he was flying with his co-pilot, Tony, a great guy and excellent pilot.

We left at 7:30 a.m. For part of the trip, I was able to fly right seat and log some of the flying time in the big twin. We made an unauthorized instrument approach, broke out over the water at 800 ft. We moved 33,000 lbs. of drill gear plus 20,000 lbs. of camp gear to Independence and Haycock. Bob, flying with Tony in the right seat, flew several big loads back and forth to the camp all night long as the camp crew and I loaded and unloaded the airplane as it came in and went out until we finished the job at 6:30 a.m. Incredible endurance of the crew, powerful roar on takeoff and break sparks off of the Skyvan on landings. We departed Omilak with last load for ANC, refueled at McGrath. Arrived at Gifford Aviation 10:30 a.m. Burned out!

We flew to the site at Nome and found that the drillers had left in the helicopter prior to our arrival, leaving their drilling equipment for us to load into the Skyvan to fly to the next camp - an expediter's nightmare. So, not only did we have to move the geological camp and the geologists with their personal gear but, all the cookware, the tents, food supplies and the geophysics gear but, now we had the extremely heavy addition of drill rods and drilling equipment. I had badly underestimated the needs of the project.

I turned to Bob Clark and his co-pilot, Tony Martin, and admitted, "I'm sorry, I'm going to have to contact the company and get another flight out here," to which he replied, "No. Let's just get the job done!"

It was like having Clutch Cargo at the wheel!

We started loading the back end of the Skyvan. The geologists were tired and a bit upset that they were asked to help move all of the drilling gear left behind. They pitched in to move their gear, but didn't touch the drilling gear belonging to drillers they worked with at every camp.

It seemed as though there ought to have been some camaraderie. I bent over and picked up a drill rod, surprised at how heavy and how grease laden it was. I made several trips; went to gather another drill rod and move it closer to the airplane prior to loading. I felt like I was in a meditative methodical trance. I moved another one, placed it and then returned to the pile to hoist up another. I was trying to be as efficient as possible for Clark, wanting his flights to the new location to get underway.

Finally, the geologists recognized they should lend a hand and came over to help. I suddenly realized some of the guys were picking up two drill rods at a time. That challenged me so I started picking up two at a time also.

We got the first of several loads into the plane and off they went.

I went on one of the runs in the Skyvan, amazed that when we opened up the door and shifted one item, the entire bottom of the Skyvan dropped onto the gravel airstrip. We were so overloaded it was unbelievable. Along with the sparks coming off the brakes, Clark's cigar glowed an incandescent red with each breath he inhaled. He was pulling long puffs in cadence with the pace of the operation.

Skyvan, Bob Clark & Tony Martin

Skyvan, supply run for HOM

161

We had to totally empty the cargo bay before taking off to return for more, and the more we worked with the drill rods, the grimier, filthier and greasier we became. When we finally returned to Anchorage, we had worked for over 24 hours non-stop, 'Arrived at Gifford Aviation at 10:30 a.m. Burnt out!'

I treated Tony Martin to a well-deserved breakfast at Peggy's Restaurant across from Merrill Field. Afterward, I went into the Captain Cook Hotel beauty shop as my hair was so coated with grease. It was styled in my usual long single braid that cascaded down to my lower back. I told the beautician, "Grab it and cut it all off!"

I then went to the fancy cigar shop in the Cook to buy a whole stack of premium cigars for Bob Clark. We shared a gratifying camaraderie from the experience. Tony enjoyed that as well as his invitation to learn more about the amazing flying in the Talkeetna area. He had been flying out of Bethel and Kotzebue and now he, another with whom I've shared some lessons in Alaska flying experiences, calls Talkeetna home.

Moving that camp location was serendipitous. To this day, Tony continues to thank Kitty for encouraging him to get acquainted with Talkeetna as a jumping-off-place for Denali expeditions. He enjoyed a great number of years later working for K2 Aviation.

Over the course of the summer, Kitty spent a lot of time in Talkeetna visiting friends. She and Roberta Sheldon would often go for long walks along the river, talking about the business of air taxis and overall life ambitions. One day, Kitty received a note from Roberta that she was to take the next day off to go flying together in her Super Cub *4023Z*. They took off, landed a few times and traded turns at the controls. After eating lunch on the gravel strip at Skwentna, a remote area on the river, they flew the 48 miles back with a bird's eye view of the spectacular scenery.

The Talkeetna Bluegrass Festival started the 11th of July. That day, Kitty arrived back from a flight to Anchorage late in the afternoon, then she and Roberta went over to the park for the great music and dancing with Kate and Holly. Just off the village airstrip in the park, the Estes Boys played with Tom Waite on banjos and fiddles, along with several other groups joining in. The music went on well into the evening. She spent the night at Roberta's, sharing her quarters with Maud the parrot.

Roberta, Hans Brunner, & Patti Skondovitch, TKA Bluegrass Festival

The following morning, Kitty, Roberta and her good friend and fellow Flying Tigers stewardess, Patty Skondovitch, headed to Talkeetna Roadhouse for coffee and their famous cinnamon rolls.

To celebrate Kitty's birthday, Kitty, Murf, and Kimball planned a luau party with the Houston Oil and Minerals camp crew in Circle Hot Springs. It would be the perfect way to lighten the guys' spirits at the end of a long, hard season "kickin rocks." To prepare, Kitty borrowed a HOM car to hit a few stores, including Woolworth's in Fairbanks. They wanted to find some fake plants and flowers to spruce-up the camp. On the way, they passed an old, local beauty shop that featured large sweeping imitation palm trees in the window. It was exactly what they needed to make the atmosphere authentically Hawaiian. They entered the store and the cheerful owner allowed them to borrow the trees for their event.

A day before her birthday, Ernestine, Kimball's mother, sent fresh Hawaiian flower leis from Honolulu. They spent that night in Fairbanks and ate dinner at The Pump House Restaurant and Saloon. The next morning, she and Murf drove 90 miles to Central with the fruit, rum and all the plastic plants. At the Central Airport, they changed into festive Hawaiian clothing. Kimball flew in from Fairbanks, landed, and they stuffed the Cessna with the plants, trees, flowers, rum, papaya and pineapples and squeezed themselves into the plane for the nine-mile flight to the Circle geology camp. They landed and handed out the fresh leis, having decorated the airplane with streamers and balloons for full effect. The cook, Lee Hart, put on a great dinner in the cook tent. After dinner, they had a Virginia Reel square dance to music from the boom box that they had also squeezed into the plane. It was a wonderful, crazy time.

As the summer of 1979 came to an end, it was time to start "demobing" the camps. Demobilizing entailed shutting down the drilling and analyzing the work required in cleaning, storing, organizing and sorting equipment in anticipation of the coming winter.

At that point, Kitty and Kimball got wind that Kenny Holland's Air Service was for sale in Talkeetna. That excited them and a great deal of conversation about some incredible possibilities ensued.

In the same burst of enthusiasm, Kimball also suggested, "Let's start our own air taxi service together, Kitty and Kimball – K2!"

Anchorage Scottish Band, K2,
Genet log building office

Bagpiper & Kitty

CHAPTER TEN

Achievement

K2 Aviation, Kitty & Kimball

Late in 1979, Kitty and Kimball purchased the Holland Air Service certificate from Ken Holland, which included a grandfather clause to operate throughout the state of Alaska. They named their new air service simply K2. Shortly afterwards, they became the co-owners of Kimball's C180 Cessna 180 *N92CP*, the first aircraft of the K2 fleet.

"You hold in your hand the camel's hair brush of a painter of Life. You stand before the vast white canvas of TIME. The paints are your thoughts, emotions, and acts. You see yourself as a builder, making a creative contribution to the evolution of modern civilization. Each moment of your life is a brush stroke in the painting of your growing career."

—Peterson

*Spring break up at
Boyd's Montana Creek Air Strip*

K2 needed an office. During March of 1980, they approached Kathy Sullivan, who had inherited a log building located in the center of town on the village airstrip, conveniently across the main street from the historic landmark Fairview Inn. The location was perfect. Their idea was to complete the building and set up offices for both K2 and Genet Expeditions in the building. Ray Genet had begun construction of the building with his mountaineering guides, but after Genet's fateful last expedition, the log building, in early construction was unfinished. In the proposition, Kitty and Kimball offered to pay for and oversee the construction in exchange for shared office space and pilot quarters in the loft. Kathy agreed and they proceeded to get it ready to move in.

Two local log builders, "Coyote," a good friend of Genet's, and Steve Hanson, finished the construction with help and oversight from Kathy, Kitty and Kimball, as promised. The building had a special character about it. The entrance featured a beautiful heavy door with a spectacular handle made from caribou antlers they found, cut and polished. The final touch to the door was a little Swiss window which had come from Genet's farmhouse in Switzerland.

Before they could move in, they still had a few things to do. The first order of business was to chase out the inhabitants; lots of birds that had taken over the loft. Then, Kathy, Kimball and Kitty cleaned it thoroughly, scrubbing all the logs and chinking with oakum so the air didn't pass through. Finally, it was ready for pilot quarters but, there was no bathroom, no water, no plumbing, no outhouse, and the first year, no heat. It was a cold, wet building with no chairs, so they sat on freshly chainsaw-cut log stumps. To top it off, there was no electricity, so they had to use a Coleman lantern for light and a three-burner Coleman for cooking. It was what they would describe as "a fairly typical Alaska domicile." The next season would be luxurious in comparison; they installed wiring for a few lights and a wood burning stove.

Just across the street, the Fairview Inn, constructed in 1923, had an illustrious history. Longtime Talkeetna musicians, Steve Durr and Doug Geeting, would often play and sing in the bar. Upstairs were several rooms, and if the walls could have talked, they would have had many stories to tell. Later, it would be said that when strong winds were blowing down the village airstrip, dictating direction of takeoff, the old timers at the bar spending good money would sober real quick as a plane roared right at them before pulling up over the rooftop.

Back in the day, there was a front door sign entering the bar that said, HIPPIES USE SIDE DOOR; the side door then had a sign that said, CLOSED. Inside there's a U-shape bar to the left, several tables and a large oak table with chairs, an old piano, a dartboard and the dustiest moose head ever to be seen anywhere.

Denali glaciers

Denali

Scott Thorburn Party: Doug, Kimball, Scott & John, First K-2 expedition

In the back room lurked a dartboard, a pool table and a barber chair. Local characters' portraits hung all around the room. Behind the bar was a big painting covering the wall; a mural of a grizzly bear high up on top of one of the ridges that overlooks Denali and the valley below.

The story goes that this grizzly is guarding Old Man Rocky Cummins' mines. Looking at the other walls, they are so yellow with nicotine that you can almost scrape it off the wall.

As the log building was being completed, K2 began a busy first season in April. Pre-booked American and German climbers arrived in town to climb Denali, which meant constant round trips to the mountain for Kitty and Kimball and the sightseeing business was also going strong. Cyndi Nelson and Scott Thorburn from Boulder were referred by Kitty to take over her job expediting with Houston Oil and Minerals in Anchorage. Prior to starting the expediting job, Scott planned a Denali expedition, guiding Doug Thorburn, his brother and John Messinen up the West Buttress. Upon their arrival to Talkeetna, they spent a few days preparing for their climb and visiting friends around town. After the plane was loaded with their expedition gear, Scott climbed aboard and said to Kimball with his ever-present grin, "Don't tell Doug and John that this is K2's first commercial glacier flight!" He then turned and waved good-bye to Cyndi.

Scott later attempted a solo assent of the Cassin Ridge while Cyndi stayed in town and became part of the family in the hanger. She was a great cook and welcome addition. While Scott was up on the mountain, she bunked up in a tent outside the hangar and made gourmet meals in her pressure cooker on a three-burner Coleman in the four-star corner kitchen area inside with the airplanes.

It wasn't surprising to see celebrities in Talkeetna, attempting anonymity, which usually didn't matter to locals anyway. It would be months later that talk would circulate about visiting musicians downing beers at the Tee Pee or Jimmy Buffett playing guitar with Doug Geeting at the Fairview Bar, or of a Hollywood swell buying bug spray at the B & K.

One who was happy to be recognized was actor Artie Johnson, the popular German soldier character on *Laugh-In,* whose signature line was, "Very interesting." At that he'd fall over on the tricycle he'd been riding.

One morning, Kitty opened the hangar door to check on her laundry drying on the Super Cub prop while Cyndi was flipping sourdough hot cakes on the griddle and there was Artie Johnson with Genet and Mike Fisher, who jokingly picked Kitty up with no warning. They all had a good laugh then they came into the hangar for Cyndi's coffee, continuing their antics.

*Kimball, C180,
Kahiltna Glacier*

As they were joking with Cyndi, Artie and Genet said they had heard that Scott was high on the mountain accompanied by a harem of women who were there to "watch over him, keep him comfortable and give him back rubs every night."

To their surprise, she said, "Oh, I hope so, and so much more." Artie and Genet were speechless with smiles of disbelief.

Climbers are awestruck upon arrival in Talkeetna to see a 20,310-foot vertical rise virtually from sea level. It is unequaled in the world, and some climbers get up to Denali, climb it, fly back to town and never see it because weather has obscured it the entire time. The mountain often stays shrouded in clouds for days. It can remain mystical to these people.

A few climbers stand out above the pack. Hans Brunner, Swiss mountain guide and good friend of Genet's, was different. One day, Kitty was struggling with a couple of 55-gallon drums of fuel, trying to roll them up to the fuel truck. He saw her wrestling these barrels and came up to

*Mike Fisher, Artie Johnson,
Kitty, & Ray Genet*

help. He was smiling at her when one of the drums shifted its weight upright and bashed into his bottom lip. It split open, gushing blood. He was going on this epic climb at serious altitude in intense sun, and now he had this big, fat, split lip. Kitty marveled at his steady temperament; he never mentioned it, he was just happy to always help out in town. Before he went on to climb, she and others celebrated with him at the Talkeetna Blue Grass Festival. Hans and his clients went on to have a successful assent up Denali, and before leaving Alaska, they expressed their gratitude.

A few weeks later, the Austrian mountaineer, Peter Habeler, walked into the K2 cabin. Habeler told Kimball he heard about K2 in Europe and had come to climb Denali and fly with K2. With that, he gave Kimball his name and said that he would like to be put on the flight schedule as soon as convenient. Kimball, not recognizing his name and thinking he looked like a sightseer, told him to go talk to the Park Service before he was going to do this intense climb.

Habeler politely replied, "Thank you very much, I will."

Kimball told Habeler that they would check the weather in the morning and give him a call to set up his flight. The next morning, Kitty got up early and headed to the "weather" hill to check out conditions en route to Denali. The ceiling was on the deck and visibility was limited.

She rode back to the log office and yelled up to Kimball in the loft, "Hey, Kimball, what's this climber's name?"

"Peter Habeler," he yelled back.

She started to dial the phone number for the hotel, stopped, and hung up. She thought, "I know that name, Habeler."

K2 Aviation, Genet Expeditions office, Village airstrip

K2 goes fishing

Kitty had a selection of books in the K2 office and pulled out Galen Rowell's *The Room of the Mountain Gods,* which he had given her. There listed was a long index on Habeler's extensive climbing expeditions. He was one of the top five climbers in the world. Among his many accomplishments was the first summit without supplemental oxygen of Mt. Everest with Reinhold Messner in 1978.

The bad weather on the mountain continued for days and the climbers could only wait it out. During this time, more climbers arrived to find that the famous mountaineer, Habeler, was in town. This created a stir and phone calls came into K2 inquiring about him.

Kimball and Kitty got to know Habeler better during several meals together. One day, while weathered-in at the Swiss Alaska Inn, Kitty checked in on him and found that he was filling out a stack of postcards. There were hundreds to be sent all over the world. She told Kimball and he suggested they make him an offer. No charge on his flights if he put their K2 Aviation stamp on his postcards. He eagerly accepted. Kitty and Kimball sat stamping postcards as he wrote them for hours at the hotel, generating future business while Mother Nature kept them on the ground.

Finally, the weather began to lift. In mid-afternoon, they capitalized on a break where there would be just a marginal opportunity to fly Habeler and his climbing partner to base camp. Kitty and Kimball loaded their gear into the C180, hoping that conditions would hold. The trip was quick. They barely got in and out. Once back in Talkeetna, delayed climbers noticed that Habeler had made it up to base camp during the bad weather. K2 was the only service that flew that day.

Denali was riddled with storms for weeks and there were many climbers in trouble. Habeler was like Spiderman on the mountain, moving quickly up and down the rugged, icy terrain rescuing others. He still made his goal to summit Denali. When he came down, Kitty and Kimball had a celebration with a special moose meat barbeque. A group of Czechoslovakian climbers joined the party and there was bluegrass music that lasted late into the night. It was a great send off.

Back in Austria, Habeler presented slideshows showing his adventurous climb. Many of the photos promoted K2 Aviation, which resulted in lots of European clientele bookings for the next season. Several of those written inquiries from Europe included a copy of Habeler's postcard with the K2 stamp on it.

On a rainy day in June, two friendly men walked into the K2 log office. They introduced themselves as the Chicago Denali team. That immediately caught Kitty's attention, as it was her hometown. They looked like they were businessmen from Chicago; they weren't your typical climbers.

Steve Fossett and his climbing partner, Dick Stockment, had prearranged a different flying service for their trip up to the base camp, but poor weather had them out exploring the town. They didn't have a guide and were unsure whether they needed snowshoes or skis for their approach at this time of year. Kitty took them to the National Park Service for a complete briefing and to review specific equipment requirements for obtaining a climbing permit.

They made the summit in just ten days, moving quickly up the West Buttress route. Then, a severe storm blew in the night after their summit and Fossett and Stockment were forced to bivouac at 17,000 feet with two other teams on their way up, an American and German team of two.

Later, Kitty sent a best wishes e-mail to Fossett while on one of his record-setting glider flights into the stratosphere, 50,720 feet, in 2006 and received a reply recalling his ascent up the West Buttress of Denali. In the e-mail, he reminisced that during his descent, he had given the German couple some chocolate before they continued their climb. Fossett and Stockment were one of the last to see the couple alive.

Kitty remembered hearing, "The German team ascended quickly. The altitude from a fast ascent caught up with them, resulting in cerebral edema." Doug Geeting was called to fly the summit area with Ranger Buchanan as soon as the weather cleared. The red tent was spotted at 17,000 feet with no visible activity. Doug continued to fly up to 19,300 feet and spotted two lifeless figures roped together. He made three passes and saw no fresh tracks.

Fossett was a wealthy financial trader who decided to pursue his adventure goals. He became a world-class climber, summiting the highest peaks on six of the seven continents. He also set records in ballooning with the first solo balloon flight around the world - a milestone in aviation history. He was the most successful speed sailor in history. In 2005, Fossett made the first solo, non-stop, non-refueled circumnavigation of the world at the controls of the Virgin Atlantic Global Flyer. He also competed in World Premier endurance sports events, including the Iditarod and Ironman Triathlon.

Fossett became an acquaintance of Kitty's and in Vail, Colorado, one evening during a dinner party at his home in Beaver Creek, he suggested that Kitty join his team of pilots. After considering the enticing offer, Kitty politely declined. By that time, her life as a mom and her business made for a full schedule.

Sadly, in September 2007, Steve Fossett disappeared during a pleasure flight over the Sierra Nevada. The search was eventually called off, even after continued private efforts. A year later, in September of 2008, a hiker found identification cards; a few days later, Fossett's crash site was confirmed.

In addition to the flurry of climbers that would come and go, there were several important people who figured into Kitty's daily schedule. One such person was Sunflower. Sunflower worked as volunteer backup radio relay, especially when weather prevented base camp transmissions. Sunflower, a lifeline for all souls connected with Mt. McKinley, was a kindly old sourdough. He lived in a cheery cabin overlooking Dahltelli Lake between the mountain and Talkeetna. In an emergency, his rich, deep voice reverberated the airways, calming panicked climbers and briefing pilots.

Without looking up, Sunflower could identify who was flying overhead just by the sound. He always knew when Kitty was flying back from the mountain because her airplane hummed gently along on its descending path. While some pilots, often under tight schedules, might continue at a quick pace to unload and pick up their next customer, she learned from Mike Fisher to always let the engine cool by throttling back on decent to land.

"Hiya, Kittyhawk, that you up there?" Sunflower would ask in his trademark Irish cadence.

"Sunflower knew how to work the radio," Don Lee recalled. "He could usually get in three or four words at a time before static would wash him out."

Sometimes the static would be so bad on Sunflower's radio that one couldn't tell if it was his wife or Sunflower himself. But as the pilots flew closer, they would attempt to pick up a clearer transmission, for Sunflower's information was often helpful.

One of Kitty's first close friends to venture north for a visit was Lili Metcalf, a longtime friend from Boulder, Colorado. Kitty spent much of her off-season time with Lili at her home, Club 519, in Boulder. Kitty had always wanted Lili to visit and to show her a good time, Alaska-style. Lili, no stranger to adventure, had brought her Klepper (three-section kayak) ready to assemble and wanted to test it out.

Ruth Glacier terminal moraine

Kitty suggested kayaking along the serpentine banks of the Susitna River with her friend, "The Woodsman." The Woodsman was a handsome maverick who made his living building cabins. He gave Lili a great taste of the Alaskan outdoors. Together, they took the Klepper down the fast, silty grey river. Lili paddled in back, The Woodsman in front, as they traveled close to the bank as a safety precaution. They reveled in the fresh Alaskan air, spotting eagle nests and beaver lodges.

Susitna River

King salmon surfaced around them as they drifted down the swift river. Suddenly, they heard a crack and saw the trees on the bank ahead start to shift. It was flood season and the rivers were running high, silently eroding their riverbanks and undermining the trees rooted in them.

As they came closer to the bank in the quick moving water, a towering cottonwood groaned, and in slow motion, heaved toward them. With a loud crack, it crashed violently into the river, just missing them and causing wild turbulence. It upheaved the Klepper as Lili and The Woodsman struggled to maintain control. The frightening ride wasn't over. A little farther down the river, the churning current had twisted the boat sideways and as they struck a concealed underwater logjam, the Klepper breached, dumping Lili and The Woodsman into the icy water. Lili remembered Kitty's warning to get to shore immediately in the case of a capsize since the freezing water instantly disables the ability to swim. Often in this situation, people get sucked under water and get entangled in branches, never to be seen again. Luckily for Lili and The Woodsman, they swam free and made it to shore.

There was a small eddy close to shore where most of their equipment was circling in the swirling water. In shock, they grabbed their things. Then, shoeless and hypothermic, they sat for a minute to get their bearings. Soaked and shivering, they began walking away from the river through the woods. Now there was a new threat: bears. Lili had heard mention that rafters die from bear attacks because bears fish along the river all summer long. Fortunately, the bears must have taken a day off from fishing this stretch of the river because they had no encounters.

They blindly trudged along in the direction of the Alaska Railroad, which paralleled the river. They walked between the rails of the tracks, and an hour later, the earth began to rumble. They moved to the side and with the rails shaking, an Alaskan flag-blue train roared toward them. Lili and The Woodsman jumped up and down and started waving. The engineer, accustomed to unscheduled stops for passengers that live up the tracks, stopped for the two wet and weary people to climb aboard. Minutes later, they were gratefully on their way back to Talkeetna.

Kitty landing hop over climbers shelter pit, Ruth Glacier

When Lili recounted her story, Kitty assured her that this much bad luck was highly unusual and with all of this over, she was going to have some fun.

"Listen. Let's go for an airplane ride," Kitty suggested to Lili a day or two later.

She figured they could spend the night at the Sheldon Mountain House for a one-of-a-kind overnight excursion in the most beautiful spot in Denali National Park above the Ruth Glacier. The cabin is located at 5,800 feet on Denali in what is known as the "Don Sheldon Amphitheater" of the Ruth Gorge. It sits perched on a spectacular five-acre granite ledge outcrop. Only feet away from the front door, the jagged rock cliff falls away to the glacier below. Sheldon built the cabin for adventure seekers such as mountaineers and photographers and to provide shelter for pilots who needed to set down in bad weather. An extraordinary pilot, he strapped huge pieces of lumber to the struts of his Super Cub and Cessna 180 and flew them to the glacier from

Talkeetna at a time when few pilots dared to take their aircraft onto the glacier at all, much less encumbered with lumber. The landing area was challenging and very bumpy with ever-changing ice fields.

Roberta Sheldon said, "The spirit of Alaska lived in that cabin!"

While touching down on the up-sloping glacier and close to 75 percent power, Kitty quickly spotted an anomaly in the center of the glacial runway. Unbelievably, some uninformed climbers had dug an underground maze of rooms smack in the middle of it. It was a multi-tiered network of mesa-like plateaus, all carved out of the glacier. Climbers were lounging on snow benches and firing up their tea on sculpted snow tables piled with cooking gear. Having already touched down on the glacier, she spotted it just in time. With a quick push on the throttle, she yanked the yoke back for lift to clear it. Lili sensed that this was not a normal occurrence.

Coming to a stop, they got out of the Cessna and onto the ice and snow airstrip. Kitty and Lili climbed the short but steep path in the snow up to the hexagonal Sheldon Mountain House overlooking a spectacular view while Kimball took the airplane back to TKA. That evening, an amazing electrical storm simultaneously scattered lightning in all directions of the compass nonstop for hours. Lili was mesmerized with the aberration.

Kitty cautioned her, "Remember, we're on a *cliff*; make sure to watch your footing when you head for the outhouse."

The nighttime dusk was punctuated by thunderous white flashes which would briefly illuminate the outhouse. Having been solidly steel-cabled to the granite for years, it was strategically positioned so that the glaciating snow would avoid it. It is directly on a precipice of a 100-plus-foot sheer vertical cliff, so a midnight trip to the outhouse took concentration for no wrong turns.

When they were scheduled for pick up, a thick fog hung on the glacier. They heard an aircraft circling above and skied down to the landing spot. As the engine sound came closer, out of the fog appeared Kimball in the Cessna 180. There was just enough clear sky above and room for him to sneak in to land. The fog rolled in again, so Lili, Kimball, and Kitty ate the dinner Kimball had brought in the plane while talking to Frances on the CB radio. When it lifted, they fired up the 180 and flew back to town.

The next day, Kitty wanted Lili to experience another adventure so she suggested she hop the next flight with their good friends to the glacier.

Lili, not particularly fond of flying in small aircraft, responded by rolling her eyes, "Sounds great." She was looking forward to forgetting her terrifying experiences thus far.

Kimball, K2 C180CP, Tokositna Glacier

Climbing friends, John Markel and Tory Stempf, had arrived in Talkeetna to climb Mt. Huntington. The mountain was named after Archer Milton Huntington, former president of the American Geographical Society and sponsor of an early expedition up the northwest branch of the Ruth Glacier. After packing the C180 with John, Tory, Lili, gear and food, Kimball flew them past impressive corniced ridges and delicate rock flutings that sweep and then enter the narrow gorge. Upon landing on the west fork of the Tokositna Glacier in less than ideal conditions with windblown snow and slightly canted touchdown area, the uphill ski broke through the crust. It dug in, causing the plane to flip tail-over-prop and come to a halt upside down. All aboard were stunned but uninjured, and they crawled out of the inverted aircraft onto the glacier.

Lili, again in a rare occurrence, wandered back from the plane trying to absorb this event and attempt to get her bearings. Just as she sat down to collect her nerves, a massive cracking sound from high up the mountain echoed in the valley and a huge avalanche began crashing down straight toward them. In shock, she reached for her camera to document what could possibly be her final moments before being snuffed out by this huge wave of churning snow. Her thoughts flashed to her cousin, who had lost his life in an avalanche just a few years before.

Lili snapped several pictures while Kimball stood stoically on the underside of the flipped aircraft's wing, facing the whirling white mass thundering down on them. To their amazement, as they braced to face the inevitable with a heavy spray enveloping them, the avalanche stopped just short, showering them in a dense cloud for several minutes. Then there was silence. The air cleared; the mountain had spared them.

Kimball got radio communication with Frances Randall on the Kahiltna Glacier and told her that they had flipped upside down on the upper Tokositna Glacier.

Randall said, "I will never forget what that was like, hearing that radio call. I kept hearing this faint message, 'This is K2, this is K2. We are upside down.' I couldn't hear clearly and I said, 'K2 upside down?'"

She was very confused. She recalled, "'Well, get right side up,' I thought.

Kimball was saying, 'This is Kimball, the airplane is upside down, we are all okay.'"

Randall got it, finally, and called Cliff Hudson, who had the highest antenna for reception. Hudson then went to tell Kitty the circumstances.

"I was deeply concerned since they were overdue and the office radio was not picking up the transmissions clearly," she remembered.

Randall, having fulfilled her duty communicating their distress, then played her violin over the radio, soothing them until Hudson arrived in the Super Cub to rescue Lili and Kimball off the glacier. The climbers, John and Tory, were undaunted and stayed on to do their climb, minus the yogurt and carrot cake that had spilled all over them in the plane during the inverted landing.

"In a matter of a few short days, Lili survived a raging river capsize, a near airplane crash, an actual airplane crash, and an avalanche," Kitty marveled.

Kitty joked that Lili should probably leave Alaska before her luck ran out. Lili, still in shock, agreed and took the first available flight out of

Anchorage and found herself in Juneau. She called between flights and said she wanted to come back up and help with their new business. Kitty thanked her and told her to keep heading south!

Lili scribbled a postcard to Kitty as she waited for her connection south: "As I sit here and get polluted in the bar on the wharf in Juneau ... with the energy you have, I know you will pull it all together and will fly high. Peanut butter sandwiches and Jack Daniels in my hip pocket for the ferry ride. Will call when I get to Seattle. To the eternal optimist and Go For It Lady! Love, Lili."

Kitty's Diary:

The damaged airplane was in Denali National Park and had to be removed. It was totaled by the insurance company because of the inaccessibility of its location, so we collected the insurance money, traded the skis for flight time, and sold the plane to our mechanic, Boyd Gochanour, owner of Susitna Air Service, who later rebuilt it, but first we had to retrieve the plane from the glacier. Flying Boyd's C180 leased to Hudson, Kimball flew in two mechanics, Larry Draveling and Boyd's son, from the Montana Creek Airstrip to the upper Tokositna to take the plane apart. They were going to spend one night and disassemble the wings and tail section the next day. They had never been up at such high altitude or remote mountainous terrain. As they worked, the weather socked in and they were stuck there for five days. On the radio, they were emphatically calling for us to get them off the mountain and trying hard to keep their language clean but their concern was obvious. On one hand, it was a bit humorous because the mountain was filled with German, Austrian, Japanese, French, Italian, and Russian climbers. Hearing all of these conversations going on when radio time is at a premium. And here are two mechanics, stuck in a snowstorm on the side of a mountain, with extreme avalanche danger at 8,400 feet hankered down with a wrecked airplane, no food and more importantly, no beer. Kimball finally flew them out when the weather cleared with the wheel skis, prop and a bunch of small heavy stuff on the back haul to the Parks Highway.

We had worked for The Houston Oil and Minerals Exploration Manager, Jim Adler, in Anchorage and he called us when seeing the article in the Anchorage Times Newspaper. He asked if we needed any help and I asked if it would be possible for one of the contracted Hughes 500D helicopters to sling out the airplane. He said it would be okay with him if it was okay with the crew chief in the area. Kimball and I flew over, radioed to the exploration camp and arranged to meet the crew chief, Greg Thurow, and his helicopter pilot alongside the Parks Highway road, where we landed in between cars on the road. Greg said it was okay with him as long as it was okay with the pilot.

Having an airplane land in front of you as you are driving is always a shock, but pilots have a way of announcing their presence with as minimal surprise as possible. From the air, pilots will always look for a large gap between cars and a straight stretch of road. As soon as Kimball landed, we quickly pulled our airplane off the highway. The challenge is in taking off, because you don't have the aerial perspective to see when the cars are coming.

The helicopter pilot, who was from Texas and green to Alaska, was chomping at the bit for a rescue attempt on Denali to pick up the bundled airfoils and assorted parts and fly them to the Parks Highway where they were to be trucked the rest of the way back to Montana Creek. Kimball and the mechanics had placed the vertical and horizontal stabilizers inside then strapped the wings along both sides of the fuselage. One big bundle!

The large dangling load began to swing at one point and had to be put down to stop it. Not exactly an easy trip. The pilot handled the challenge well and did a great job.

We asked the helicopter pilot what we owed him and he smiled, requesting a bottle of Jack Daniels. We also asked Jim at HOM what we owed for the helicopter time and he replied, "What helicopter time?"

The situation was full of humor, tragedy, and caring. Everyone chipped in to help. Kimball and I wanted to be in the air taxi business but this, wow, this was a more difficult start than expected.

It was all the support from Roberta Sheldon, climbers and everyone in Talkeetna that pulled us through. Cliff Hudson loaned us his airplane and had us picking up his clients along with ours and I got busy flying float trips for him.

It was a turning point. Everyone was saying, "K2 has to stay in there."

For the rest of the season, Kitty stayed busy flying the C185 floatplane for Cliff Hudson while Kimball flew climbers to Denali in Cliff's C185. Both had time to reflect on the startup of K2 and the obstacles they had encountered while holding strong to their determination to fulfill their dream.

In August, they signed a contract with Ken Holland to buy his Cessna 185 *N1292F*, "*Red Fox.*" It would become an iconic addition to K2's future identity. The bold red workhorse plane with a boisterous roar on takeoff would become the centerpiece of K2 Aviation for years to come.

The season wrapped up as the end of September approached and the population of Talkeetna dwindled until it was just the locals who called the special place home. They would greet each other at the post office or at the B & K as they quietly began to prepare for the harsh winter.

Kimball and Kitty headed south toward the lower 48, flying *Red Fox* through Canada to Watson Lake, Yukon, Edmonton, Alberta, Moose Jaw, Saskatchewan, then Minneapolis and on to her destination, Chicago.

During a visit to Chicago, Kitty flew the Cessna 185 often, making short trips up to Wisconsin for breakfast with her father, Jack. His enthusiasm was always contagious. He loved airplanes and flying with his children and he would always be ready for a trip in the sky. Kitty and her dad were already close, but the flight time together became some of their most special shared memories.

During the fall and winter months, Kitty and Kimball kept busy focusing on setting up the 1981 K2 season. There was a lot of work to be done. They drummed up clientele and made bookings for the business through writing letters and making phone calls, which was an important part to making the upcoming climbing season a success.

Tory Stempt, John Markel, & Kimball,
Tokositna Glacier, Lili Metcalf photo

*Tokositna Glacier Landing, avalanche,
Kimball, Lili Metcalf photo*

K2, K2, where do you roam?
Can you take us to the Moose's Tooth,
A place that is far from home?

We've come to conquer the East face,
We tell some passers-by.
They smile, for they do not know
It's nearly one mile high.

We landed on the Buckskin Glacier,
Not a crevasse in sight.
I'm glad it's over, the journey I mean
It was a nerve-wracking flight.

We pitched our tents upon the snow
And there we were **doomed** to stay,
For the snow it did swirl around
From that moment up to this day.

It was on the Buckskin Glacier,
The snow was in the air.
Kitty said that she'd come in
As soon as it was clear.

The snow it fell thick and fast,
The food was running thin.
But we just sat there waiting
For Kitty to come in.

The wind and snow did flurry,
We were in a sorry plight.
Come on Kitty, come on in
Give us a flight, tonight.

The Moose's Tooth did stand behind
Towering one mile high.
Come on Kitty, take us home
To some home-made apple pie.

Alas, alas, what will be the end?
We are still here, is this day ten?
Come on Kitty, don't be shy,
Come on Kitty, let's fly.

Fly,

Fly.

~Graham Mercer
Scottish climber
May, 1980

Poem for Kitty,
by Graham Mercer, Scottish Climber

*Kitty & Gary Bocarde in
K2 shirt, Kahiltna Glacier*

*K2 Art
by Mary Murphy*

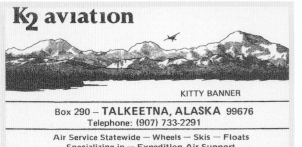

Bob Fulton, Kahiltna Glacier,
Edgar Boyles photo

Float fishing with Lulu, Clarence Lake

CHAPTER ELEVEN

Leadership

Kitty's log book & schedules

"The leader does not say, 'Get going!' Instead, he says, 'Let's go!' and leads the way. A leader is a self-starter: creating plans and setting them in motion; both a person of thought and a person of action – both dreamer and doer, one who glorifies the team spirit."

—Peterson

After months of scheduling and marketing, K2 Aviation began the 1981 season in early April with a booked-up roster of flights to the glaciers of Denali.

During the busy season, climbers provided both an endless supply, and conversely, a drain of energy. The two K2 owners were involved with them daily and did their best to provide support in any way they could. Upon arrival in Talkeetna, the climbers were full of fire, enthusiastic about their imminent climbs and goals of conquest. If the weather was not cooperating, which was frequent, and they were unable to fly up to base camp, their energy would sometimes shift to frustration. Ascending the mountain posed continuous challenges, including treacherous steep terrain, unpredictable weather, and freezing temperatures. Descending the mountain was equally difficult. Often while on the mountain, climbers would get frostbite and pilots would have to fly in to pick them up and take them to the hospital in Anchorage. Dr. John Mills, a frostbite specialist at Providence Hospital, had a state-of-the-art frostbite chamber for treating his patients.

"*Kahiltna International*"

When the weather was down, cooking and sharing food together as a group was one of the best ways to distract the climbers from their anxious waiting. It was also a good opportunity for them to spend quality time and make new friends in Talkeetna.

A group of climbers from Germany had been waiting several days for the weather to clear. Kitty, in an attempt to keep their spirits up, charged them with the job of building a picnic table for

K2 headed to Denali

the front yard of the K2-Genet building. Kathy led them to a pile of logs left over from the construction of the building and showed them where the tools and chainsaws were. They took to the project with zeal and in a matter of hours created a beautiful log table dovetailed and complete with their carved initials. Proud of their accomplishment, they sat at it playing cards and eating a leftover moose-meat feast from the night before, waiting for the weather to break.

Many friends in town fished the mighty rivers and brought home trophy catches, especially Nancy and Mac on their riverboat outings with clients. They were eager to share with Kitty and Kimball's climbers and join in on the fun for a salmon bake. From river to grill, the taste of fresh-caught, wild Alaskan salmon is unforgettable. If someone in town had extra moose meat, they would join in and cook it up and the aroma would waft through the tents. Suddenly, a line of climbers holding tin camp plates would appear. We made the meals jump with color and extra Alaskan by tossing freshly picked bluebells, wild-roses, and berries into the salad.

Refueling, C185 92F

One year, the Talkeetna Miner's Day Festival featured a shooting contest. After landing from a flight, Kitty heard the buzz about the tournament, and with a few minutes to spare between flights, jumped into the truck and motored over to where the shooting was in progress.

"I was handed the local Veteran of Foreign Wars shotgun by Ace Ebling and Jim Okonek spun the target. I aimed and fired and ended up with the most shot in the target, luckily not spraying Jim with any lead! I was now the proud winner of one large turkey," she recalled, smiling.

Driving back to the airport she shouted to a group of climbers she'd just flown back. The exhausted Polish climbers didn't speak much English, so she gestured shooting a gun, flapped her arms like a bird, rubbed her tummy, and the climbers, hungry for some real food, quickly

Doug Geeting, One Shot Pass

figured it out. Kitty scribbled directions to where they could pick up the turkey, hopped into the Cessna and then disappeared in a cloud of runway dust. The suddenly motivated climbers embarked on the adventure of trying to find this 'bird' that she had shot, not knowing it was a frozen turkey prize. At the end of the bustling day, she found the climbers in the front yard of the K2-Genet log office. They had just roasted the turkey over the 55-gallon oil drum that had been converted into an Alaskan-style grill and were waiting for Kitty, Kimball and Kathy so everyone could dig in.

One morning in late April, Kitty flew two base camp radio gals to the glacier. As she approached One Shot Pass, the engine began to run rough. She increased the power slightly and adjusted the mixture as she continued the flight over the pass and up to the glacier, thinking it could just be the gain in altitude. She was scanning the heavily crevassed glacier field below for an emergency landing spot, but continued on and set up her approach for touchdown on the Kahiltna. Before leaving for the return, she did her run up and the engine seemed to run smoothly. Back in Talkeetna, Kitty told Mike Fisher about the incident. Fisher looked at the Cessna 185 with her and checked for water in the fuel. They even checked the fuel truck tank and found no water anywhere. He surmised that it was induction icing and alerted the Anchorage FAA office. A notice was sent out that injected engines are not immune from this problem. Many pilots think that only carbureted engines have icing issues; which is not the case.

Kitty flew supply trips in and out of remote gold and ore mines. The miners were forever embroiled in territorial disputes, eternally at their neighbors' throats. Not realizing the depth of these disagreements, Kitty, while flying the mining routes, unknowingly became a pawn in the constant conflicts. A certain miner even threatened to shoot Kitty and Kimball down if he saw them delivering supplies to his adversary.

Caribou

One notable incident was when K2 received an urgent radio request from a miner pleading that they fly quickly to a certain mine for a pick up and immediate air evacuation. He urgently stated that there had been a death threat toward him and that his family's lives were in danger. They had hit a "glory hole" (an unbelievable rich deposit of gold) and other miners in the area had become aggressive. His desperation to get out right away was clear as he gave K2 his location. When Kimball and Kitty arrived, the man, his wife and two kids were anxiously waiting as they shut the engine down.

One child was wearing only one shoe. They carried only a pillowcase filled with their belongings, (or perhaps a gold stash). Kitty and Kimball quickly boarded the frightened family and delivered them to Talkeetna. After paying for the flight, they left and were never seen or heard from again.

That summer, K2 was presented an excellent opportunity. They signed a contract with Alaska Fish & Game to track the distance salmon traveled up the Susitna River for spawning from July to September. The fish were being tracked for a feasibility study to provide a background document for salmon resource investigations relative to the proposed Susitna Hydroelectric Project. It was a busy schedule, with regular early morning flights along the river and more flying later in the day. Salmon were radio tagged by Fish & Game at the old-style Indian Yukon Fish Wheel in the upper Susitna River. Fish wheels function like paddlewheels, using the current of the river to rotate sampling baskets which capture salmon as they migrate up river through turbid rivers. Two Fish & Game biologists flying with K2 above the fast-moving rivers then monitored progress of the fish.

Kitty flew the Devil's Canyon route just north of Talkeetna as they followed the Susitna River, home to the salmon and major producer for the Cook Inlet Fishery. The government hoped to dam the river for the hydroelectric power, but it was not a popular proposal among the Talkeetna population. Devil's Canyon is one of the last natural wild rapids in the northern hemisphere. Opponents argued that damming it would be another nail in the environment's coffin. It would disrupt the salmon, who needed to reach their point of origination for spawning to complete their lifecycle.

Roberta Sheldon was instrumental in fighting the proposed Susitna Dam Project. As recently as 2012, she was on record against the dam, writing in *The Mat-Su Valley Frontiersman*: "Some might think that a dynamite river with Alaska-caliber fish runs, together with a small, entrepreneurial town with a strong work ethic and economy, are worth sacrificing for an exorbitantly priced dam. Or that the health of almost countless named and unnamed tributaries and side-sloughs that harbor spawning salmon from the mouth of Cook Inlet to the proposed dam site doesn't count. Don't bet on it."

On the other side of the debate, the pro-developers argued that it was impossible that any type of fish could make it alive through the un-rated whitewater, therefore tracking the fishes' progression would prove evidence either way.

Kitty was guided to the fish by the faint beeping noise bouncing off antennas attached to the wing struts, flying farther and farther up the river to track 14 salmon. The biologists assigned names to the lead fish. Each day as the fish neared the whitewater, they cheered them on and bet for their favorites.

On one trip the tracking signal that they had been following veered out of the river and up a mountain. After a little thought, everyone laughed and realized a bear had just had a happy meal. On another trip, the weather was deteriorating in classic Alaskan fashion and the Fish & Game biologists almost decided to forgo a risky flight. But Kitty thought the weather would hold and reasoned that they needed to keep constant tabs on the fish, especially this close to the whitewater. The fish were at a crucial point, nearing Devil's Canyon's un-rated whitewater.

They took off, racing ahead of the weather. Engrossed with the excitement of finding the fish, they didn't look back until it was time to turn around. They saw the weather closing in fast; the clouds had dropped and moisture bullets began to rivulet up the windshield. Kitty reduced altitude to avoid the grey, wet mass. She radioed Talkeetna Flight Service to learn that the cloud ceiling was below minimum for visual landing but was given a "special VFR" from Revis at the FSS to land at the Talkeetna Airport.

"The Fish & Game guys knew the river like the back of their hands, so we flew right above it and they helped navigate," Kitty remembered. "The ceiling lifted a bit and I could see Talkeetna, so I headed for the airport. We landed just in time since the weather dropped below minimums and no one was able to fly in or out for the rest of the day."

They eventually tracked the salmon and found that they made it all the way up Devil's Canyon to spawn. The research findings were used to support the decision to terminate the dam project.

Kitty was happy to have her parents finally visit her new Alaska digs. She invited them to come to Talkeetna and see for themselves this wild and wonderful place that she exuberantly described in letters. They looked forward to flying with their daughter in Alaska. She met them in Anchorage and took them on a bus tour bus to Valdez, where they hopped on a ferry to see the Columbia Glacier in Prince William Sound, one of the fastest moving tidewater glaciers flowing directly into the sea.

It was spectacular to see high chunks of ice calve off the terminus of the glacier. When they arrived back in Anchorage, Kitty's mother looked at her and said, "Please, whatever you do, I don't want to fly in bad weather."

They all settled in the Cessna 185 with groceries and bags stuffed all around them. Kimball was flying, circling and pointing out moose. Helen did not enjoy uneven flight attitudes in an airplane, especially low-level ones. After landing, they stuffed their bags in the back of the old pickup truck and stuffed themselves into the front seat. After checking her parents into the Talkeetna Motel, they headed to town to meet Roberta Sheldon, Mike, Susanne and other local friends.

The next day, weather prohibited flying. Mac Stevens, a master river guide, invited Kitty and her folks to take a riverboat ride up the Talkeetna River to show them the sights. Kimball, Kathy Sullivan, her four-year-old son Taras and her two-year-old Adrian all boarded the riverboat with Kitty and her parents. Several miles up the river, the boat's engine started to sputter. It choked out a few dying gasps and then unceremoniously conked out. Everyone looked at Mac. He immediately turned the key, attempting a restart. No ignition. He keyed it again. Nothing.

The boat started drifting backwards. Mac glanced at the fuel level and other instruments. Rapidly troubleshooting, he repetitively turned the key. Now skimming rapidly backwards, the boat was gathering speed in the rushing cold water. They saw logjam after logjam.

"I looked at my mom and she was still nervously smiling, not a great swimmer, but we would kid her saying she was a hell of a side-stroker. Dad had been a lifeguard and suggested we get the life jackets on." Kitty remembered, "Kimball jumped to action, removed the engine cover and began pulling parts off looking for trouble spots, moving so quickly he cut his fingers."

Suddenly, they realized they were heading straight at an ominous log jam. Everyone braced for impact. You don't want to hit the logs sideways or you can breach and flip. Kathy charged to the back of the boat in two steps, wielding a wooden oar. Extending the oar with her long arms, she thrust it against the logs, shoving the boat away. Kimball continued working on the engine. Out of nowhere, a Fish & Game Zodiac pulled up next to them and assessed the situation, jockeyed their boat behind the hampered craft, and shoved it into a shallower area. Kimball figured that there was water in the gas so he flushed the system, saving the day. Mac turned the key and the engine fired up.

With the engine now running again, Kitty wanted to show her parents the Fish & Game old-style Indian Yukon Fish Wheel a bit farther up the river. They tied up and hiked through the thick woods to where the enormous wooden fish wheel was scooping up fish and sliding them into a holding area. The wheel turning with the rhythm of the river.

"My parents had an eventful first day in the wilds," Kitty said, "and they were still smiling", back at the Latitude 62 having a beer with Nancy Trump.

In Alaska, you live by the weather. Three days later, the sun came out. Kitty guessed that they could finally get up to Denali so she loaded her parents into the C185 with her dad sitting right seat and her mom behind him. They took off from the tree-lined, dirt village airstrip, and noticing that her mom had dug her nails into her father's shoulder, Kitty asked her how she was doing.

With her voice raised a couple octaves, she replied, "Fine!"

Finally, Jack, almost bleeding from Helen's nails gripping his shoulder, turned to Kitty and said, "We had better take her back."

Kitty made a steep bank and headed for the state airport just out of town. After they touched down and finally stopped without shutting down the engine, she let her mom out and pointed the way to the cabin in the woods, about a block from the landing site.

Kitty said to her, "Walk fast and get in the cabin. We'll be back to pick you up."

Off went Helen in giant steps. When Jack asked why she insisted that Helen close the cabin door, Kitty replied, "The area has bears, wolves, moose and dogs - big ones."

When Kitty could see that her mom reached the cabin, they took off for Denali for a short, scenic ride. Kitty was hoping that there would be enough clear sky to possibly catch a view of Denali as they flew up the terminal moraine of the Kahiltna Glacier. They caught a glimpse, but weather didn't cooperate for a glacier landing so they returned to the airport to go meet Helen.

Kitty spent time showing her parents around Talkeetna. They hit all the hot spots, starting with the Three Rivers Union 76 gas station where she took her showers and did her laundry. The place was always busy since all the climbers used the facility. The highlight of any morning was the Talkeetna Roadhouse for its great breakfast and the incredible giant cinnamon rolls. This stop was a home run since Jack had a sweet tooth and Helen loved their strong homebrew coffee. A late stop at the 'Ol Fairview Bar made their day.

She walked them to the river, hoping to catch a glimpse of Denali, which could be seen on a clear day jutting toward the sky from this spot. Again, low, grey clouds obscured the iconic mountain.

In late July, with her parents still in town, Kitty, Kimball and Kathy invited Ed Homer and Sandy to marry in the K2-Genet log cabin. They moved their log stump seats and desk out of the way and cleaned the cabin up nicely for the wedding party. Helen joined the others and picked fireweed and beautiful wild flowers, decorating the cabin inside and out. Jack got a good fire going in the wood-burning stove to warm up the damp air.

Father Ron Dunphey, Catholic priest loved by all, performed a wonderful service. Doug Geeting and Tom Waite played lively bluegrass music as Sandy and Ed made their way out of the cabin and through the mud puddles on route to the Fairview for some fun. Then the married couple departed the celebration in a helicopter that awaited them out front on the village airstrip. Before flying off into marital bliss, they made a low pass with "Just Married" cans dragging on the main street.

Now that Helen and Jack had seen where their daughter was living and experienced some of the flying, they were content to head back to Chicago. One of Kimball's friends, a helicopter pilot who had flown the Houston Oil and Mineral camps while Kimball was there, offered to take them down to Anchorage. But Helen had experienced enough "bush" flying on this trip, and once again, the weather wasn't perfect. She didn't know what to expect and reluctantly stepped up to enter the cockpit of the two-seat helicopter as Jack pushed her inside.

Seated and belted between the pilot and Jack, Helen called out to Kitty with a smile on her face, "I'll meet you at the Captain Cook Bar!"

With that they were up and away. Kitty imagined that she must be awfully nervous in the bubble canopy of the helicopter flying over the tundra and crossing low over the Cook Inlet. When Kimball and Kitty arrived at the Captain Cook in Anchorage, toting luggage, they found Jack, Helen and the pilot laughing and having a great time. They had been celebrating with drinks-several they had guessed. Helen loved her new form of transportation and the sensation of the chopper. The pilot really enjoyed her parents and even sent them a Christmas card.

An important part of the business was reading and writing letters. At that time, planning the schedules for summer was done almost completely by postal mail. This was complicated by the fact that many climbers were coming from all over the world. They had to plan this stuff months and months in advance. The climbers would send letters requesting flights to the mountain on certain dates. Kitty would write back with instructions to send deposits, and the climbers would write back with the deposits - all through international mail.

Kitty remembered, for example, receiving a mysterious letter addressed simply to: Kitty Banner, Bush Pilot, Talkeetna, Alaska. It notified her that a couple was going to be out in the woods doing a kayak trip. They wanted a pickup at a certain location on the northeast side of a specific lake on a specified date and time. The letter warned this was the only notice Kitty would receive. They were leaving, and as they would be away for a full month, they admitted there would be no further correspondence.

"Since I was flying floats for Cliff Hudson at the time and the letter didn't go to Cliff, I had to tell him I'd been asked to pick up two kayakers. Receiving letters of this nature was not uncommon. Sometimes this was the only way of communication to set up the pick-up flight. However, with no confirmation, it's pretty expensive to fly the floatplane to just hope that somebody shows up," she remembered. "The day arrived on the flight schedule and the weather posed no problems. I flew to the lake on the requested date and time, circled an overhead air search looking for them from above, but didn't see anybody. I thought I'd set down and just wait for a bit."

She made a water landing and floated there apprehensively. Forty-five minutes passed. There are always so many variables that could affect the hikers' pick-ups. Suddenly, a man and woman showed up out of the bush with their foldable kayak. As Kitty loaded their gear, she asked, "How did you get my name?"

They said they had heard of her, but she thought it was pretty amazing they would have faith that she would just show up. The man shrugged his shoulders and said, "I just thought you would come."

Kitty asked where they were from. They told her they were paid picketers for the Rocky Flats Nuclear Site in Boulder, Colorado. Coincidence since Kitty was spending her winters in Boulder. She loaded their gear, got them on board and flew back to Talkeetna.

Kimball Forrest at K2 office

Ken Taylor, state of Alaska wildlife biologist for Fish & Game, noted, "It's easy to remember Kitty's birthday is September 1st. It marks the first day of duck hunting season in Alaska."

Kitty's most memorable birthday celebration was a surprise party hosted by Kathy Sullivan at her Genet Cabin on the Talkeetna River. Kathy asked Kimball Forrest to distract Kitty with a river raft trip, and while the duo floated lazily down the 'Big Su,' Kathy and her partners in crime outdid themselves with clever arrangements. A piano bedecked with a candelabra that would have amazed even Liberace was hauled through the woods to Kathy's front yard and people arrived in the stealthy manner for the celebration.

It had been a rainy summer but the sky was bright with sunshine for the first time. Everyone rushed to get out and enjoy good weather. Early in the morning, Kitty went to the airport and flew a spectacular scenic flight up to the mountain and then stopped at the post office to pick up a birthday package from her mom. It contained a pound cake and a bottle of perfume.

"I left the bottle top intact," she said. "Not a good idea to use in Alaska. You'd attract every mosquito within miles."

Kitty took the package to the Fairview, where the older local gals were having their afternoon coffee seated around the bar. They loved the perfume and sprayed each other and ate the pound cake with giggles and smiles. Then, Kimball and Kitty bought a six-pack for a float on the river. They never touched the oars, drifting like two people in a tub going round and round.

"Denali seemed to be jumping out of the water that day because you're flat on the river at 350 feet above sea level and the mountain is right there, a straight vertical rise to 20,310 feet," she remembered.

They later headed to what Kitty believed to be a small roof-raising party at Kathy's cabin. As they turned and walked down the wooded drive toward the cabin, she was startled to see through the trees and tall fiddlehead ferns half the town's population. They were gathered around a piano and there sat a traveling music man, Johnny B, decked out in a tuxedo and top hat. All their voices came together as he pounded out a dramatic "Happy Birthday."

"I just stood there while everyone belted out 'Happy Birthday' and the alpenglow cast a golden aura. It was surreal, like out of a Fellini movie," Kitty remembered.

Holly & Kate Sheldon, silver salmon catch

Later that evening at the campfire, the local architect, Murray Nash, played his saxophone while Kitty's young friend, Cecelia Arett, blasted a bugle. Kitty, the center of attention, was delighted to receive several typically Alaskan gifts. She received a moose tooth necklace from Suzanne and Mike Fisher. Suzanne had set out to make Jellied Moose Nose, a traditional and time-honored Alaskan dish of real sliced moose snout made from a boiled moose head. During the boiling process, all the moose teeth popped out, so Fisher strung Kitty a moose tooth necklace. Other gifts included a hand-woven Aleut basket, feather hairpieces, and Big Su River sand people baked and painted by Kate Sheldon.

They feasted on barbequed moose meat, salmon and an array of potluck dishes along with a healthy dose of spirits. Kate frosted a picture of the K2 Cessna 185, *Red Fox*, on a birthday cake. As the sun circled the horizon, the silver candelabra atop the piano lit up the scene. A bonfire roared and flickered below and the northern lights began to dance above. No one wanted the evening to end.

The best part of hunting season was visiting all the lakes. At least half of Kitty's visits to the lakes were first time landings. "It's autumn, the tundra is turning gold and red, and the quiet remoteness is so peaceful. You'd hop out onto the spongy, springy moss with hidden berries. Ice is in the air, it's so clean and clear," she remembered.

In the fall at Stephan Lake, Kitty would take a sauna at the lodge and then break through the thin ice into the lake. "I'd be mesmerized looking up at the stars and northern lights, it's spectacular," she said. After first snowfalls, she enjoyed lying in a snow bank watching the northern lights quietly transform the sky.

Once she was transporting a couple of older gentlemen from Anchorage who, for several years, had been moose hunting the same Stephan Lake area. It was the first time they had a female bush pilot and Kitty noticed they had the not uncommon nervous apprehension. She greeted the men then fueled the floatplane and pumped the water out of the floats. Loading her passengers and their gear, she slid into the pilot's seat. She fired up the engine, ran through her checklist, and taxied down the lake for takeoff. After a quick flight, they soon landed on the northeast shore of Stephan Lake. Soon after unloading the plane, the hunters began filling their inflatable kayaks and putting together paddles with distinctive large white tips. Kitty confirmed their pickup date, wished them good luck, and took off.

They honored the "same day rule," and the next morning while paddling across the lake, a huge bull moose spotted them. The moose was intrigued with the motion of the paddles, which resembled another bull moose treading through water. It quickly made its way down to protect his turf and the hunters hit the bonanza. The big bull was theirs. After dressing out the moose and hanging the meat, they rested easy until Kitty's scheduled pick up.

"The bull was so big that it took up an entire load, with the head next to me on the floor." Kitty laughed, "It was the first time that I had a moose head as a copilot!"

When unloading their bounty from the plane on the second run, they insisted Kitty join them at the Fairview Inn Bar for a cocktail. She knew better than to order a beer. Instead, she would order a single shot of Yukon Jack. A toast was made as they expressed their appreciation and amazement at Kitty's piloting skills. She smiled, raised her glass, and as they tipped their heads back to drink, she tossed her drink over her shoulder onto the wall. Through the years, the wall behind where Kitty usually sat developed an extra layer of liquor lacquer.

One day, pilot Cliff Hudson and his wife, Ollie, invited Kitty over to a cocktail reception honoring a group of Japanese clients. The event was held in Hudson's Quonset hut in a newly added upstairs room. As Kitty entered, she was surprised to see a large group of Japanese climbers and entourage. She took a seat among them.

"They were older, esteemed men, most of whom didn't speak much English," Kitty said.

She sat down with another pilot, Ed Homer. They all talked and communicated as best possible while sipping at the special sake they had brought along. After a while, the most senior Japanese man smiled and began to address Kitty. The room quieted. This man was important, revered by everyone there.

He looked at her and said, "You will marry a big man."

Trying to understand, she nodded and motioned a tall person.

The man shook his head and replied, "Not big in stature, but man with big heart."

Kitty smiled brightly, noting his sincerity and wisdom.

After Kitty and Kimball buttoned things up for the winter off-season, they flew *Red Fox* south for the long trip through Canada and on to the lower 48.

Kitty, tie down Red Fox, Galen Rowell photo

Kitty climbing, Galen Rowell photo

CHAPTER TWELVE

Being

"Is knowing that when we move into the future it becomes the now, and that now is the appointed time."

—Peterson

In the spring of 1982, Kitty began working on her glider rating at The Cloud Base at the Boulder Airport. Wind and weather can cause problems for a pilot, and from the first introductory flight, all must learn how much wind affects an aircraft.

A new pilot learns to respect the wind strength and direction to determine takeoff and landing runways or to plan for crosswind techniques, slips to landings, to maintain directional control. Reading signs on the earth's surface gives clues: wind socks, flags straining against their poles, ripples on water, smoke rising, and snow being blown clear of mountain peaks give clear messages of wind direction, turbulence, and strength. Soaring in a craft that cannot be powered out of tight circumstances or sharply pitched or banked also sharpens piloting skills. Learning to fly a glider in mountainous terrain taught a greater appreciation and knowledge of these invisible forces. There is a unique exhilaration to flying such as a bird riding up drafts to gain altitude and soaring in silence without an engine.

In 1982, Kitty received her glider pilot certificate. In addition to glider flight training with Chris Hubert at The Cloud Base in Boulder, she made another more difficult decision. She and Kimball sold K2 to Jim Okonek, a local Talkeetna pilot and retired Lieutenant Colonel from Elmendorf Air Force Base in Anchorage. Jim first came to Alaska in 1964 with his wife, Julie, as a helicopter pilot working at the Rescue Coordination Center for the U.S. Air Force. His son, Brian, was an accomplished climber on Denali and the Alaska Range and Okonek would fly him to the mountain.

Kimball wanted to return to academia to convert his geological research into a PhD dissertation and work toward a career in geology. He had asked that if they ever sold K2, they would do it together. Kitty, honoring his request, was also ready for a change, but not entirely ready to give up flying in Alaska. She felt there would be more to come. Together, they had persevered through many obstacles and made a huge imprint in Alaska's illustrious flying history.

Selling K2 was not easy for Kitty. She had worked so hard to achieve her dream of owning and operating her own air taxi service in Alaska. She truly loved Talkeetna and the town's special blend of people, many who became close friends and whom remain in touch to this day. Moving on from that powerful dream was bittersweet. But Kitty would now have more time to pursue other projects.

That summer, an independent CBS Executive Producer, Robert Smith Kiliper, contacted her about the possibility of doing a screenplay for a TV movie. He discovered her after reading an article in *The Chicago Tribune*. She met him in Minneapolis for a voice taping. Soon after, Kitty and Kiliper traveled extensively throughout Alaska recording transcripts about her flying experiences and events, along with the geography, history, and culture of the region.

She was then invited to California to meet with Kiliper and Norman Powell, the Executive Producer of CBS' *Made for TV Movies*. There she met with CBS writers Tom Lazarus and William Schwartz and developed two separate screenplays. Kitty recommended that the producers consider shooting the movie in Washington State to save on production costs. She noted that the small towns she had studied as alternate landing sites in her early pilot training could "feel" like Talkeetna.

The movie was never produced, but when Northern Exposure later became a TV series, the similarities appeared to be more than coincidental. The little town of Roslyn, Washington, was selected for filming to represent the "quirky" fictional town of Cicely, Alaska.

According to the *Alaskan Talkeetna Times*, "Talkeetna, a distinctive community of less than 500 is often said to be the inspiration behind the television series, *Northern Exposure*."

As for Kitty, publicity surrounding Kitty's bush piloting role in Talkeetna seems perfectly suited to having sowed the idea of a woman Alaskan bush pilot as central to a television mini-series in the minds of the creators of the show. Several elements of *Northern Exposure* included features from the treatments that she had worked on with the CBS writers while she was under contract with CBS in 1982 and 1983. Most notable were the revisions that her father, Jack Banner, made to those early treatments.

This biography, however, is not a fictional account of Kitty Banner Seemann. It celebrates the highly competent and capable glacier and bush pilot, and the many episodes and predicaments in which such an appealing and adventurous woman in an untamed, demanding locale can become involved. Intriguingly, in raw and wild Alaska, Kitty's actual flights were by far more challenging and dangerous than those represented in the show, confirming that reality can be vastly more compelling than film or television.

In truth, Kitty had lost her fair share of mentors and friends in aviation who were also following their dreams and passions. They left an indelible mark on her life in aviation.

She learned valuable inspiration and inner journey having shared, not only their friendship, but their spirit and love of adventure to take aviation to a higher level.

"I honor their lives and deaths and know that fate plays a role when one pushes the envelope. I am grateful that God was my co-pilot and that I live on celebrating life to its fullest and know those, not here now, helped enrich my spirit for aviation and life itself."

Most notably:

✈ Professor David Rahm, the remarkable pilot who taught her to fly.

✈ John Denver, who obtained training for his floatplane rating from Kitty, in Alaska.

✈ Steve Fossett, outstanding aviator and adventurer.

✈ Robert "Bob" Fulton of Aspen, Colorado, cinematographer and pilot who won an Emmy News and Documentary Award for *Denali: Alaska's Great Wilderness*. Kitty flew his C180 with Fulton filming the Little Switzerland sequence for an Alaskan documentary.

Galen Rowell, internationally known wilderness photographer and photojournalist with numerous assignments for *National Geographic* and author of many beautiful, large-format books of photos and text. He was a legend among mountain climbers. Galen knew the compelling lure of Alaska and was a close friend to a young Kitty Banner. Rowell wrote, "Her future now lies with the winds of the world, and the *wings of her dreams*."

Bob, Kahiltna, Alaska

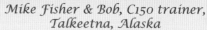

Mike Fisher & Bob, C150 trainer,
Talkeetna, Alaska

Sept/1/84
Talkeetna AK

Dear Kitty,
  It has been a great summer, good
gardens, lots of blue berries & sunshine.
I think most businesses made money.
Looks as though we'll have a beautiful
autum. But, as somebody mentioned
the other day, "What good is a great
summer & beautiful autum without
Kitty Banner?", "It's like being all dressed
up and nowhere to go". miss ya, John Carlson

John Carlson note to Kitty

MCWILLIAMS MINE – 1983

Long final

Short final

Take-off position

"Mac"

Cook tent

Airstrip

Kitty at John Ireland's cabin, Murder Lake, 1985

Stephan Lake Lodge sauna cabin

Kitty & John Ireland, fishing,
John Denver shoot

CHAPTER THIRTEEN

Living Forever

Bob & Kitty in Cub on Katie Lake

"Your example, your words, your ideas, your ideals can be projected into the future to live forever in the lives of others."

— Peterson

In 1982, Kitty met Bob Seemann in Vail, Colorado, soon after a story on her ran in *Outside* magazine. He had been a championship ski racer out of New England, manager for the Rossignol Professional Team, 1973-'74, Vail Town Champion 1977, head alpine coach for Ski Club Vail, and at the time, a sales representative in Colorado for Olin Ski Company.

A coworker of Bob's who had met Kitty in Winter Park, was staying with him. He told Bob about Kitty, calling her a "cute, really friendly, Alaska glacier pilot." Bob was preparing dinner, as he walked in and *the* magazine was open to the article about Kitty on the kitchen counter. Bob asked, "is this her?" The answer was "yes."

They were invited to meet Kitty and her friends to ski at Beaver Creek the next day. With a big ski group, Bob and Kitty didn't really talk much; that is, not until they rode a chair lift alone together. Kitty asked Bob if he had ever been to Alaska. He asked if she knew of Katie Lake, only 16 miles by float plane from Talkeetna. He told her that in 1969, he, his dad, sister and brother-in-law, had homesteaded four, five-acre parcels of land, on the lake.

Kitty, surprised, remembers he jokingly stated, "'We bought the property a few years before you went to Alaska.'" And after a pause, "Bob told me that he was a subscriber to *Outside*."

Bob had also driven the Alaskan Highway several times and had worked on a fishing tender out of Anchorage in 1969. His sister, Mimi, and brother-in-law, John Morton, a U.S. Team biathlete and Olympian, had lived in Anchorage for years.

That evening, Kitty and Lili had planned a small dinner party and invited Bob. They talked that evening about Alaska and found common interests in so many things. But, it would be a year before they would see or talk to one another again. Soon after, Kitty headed to Alaska to work on the CBS project with Bob Kiliper.

A year later the two would reconnect and this reacquaintance lit a spark.

Kitty invited Bob to Lili's Easter brunch at her home in Boulder. It was a yearly event with the Boulder String Quartet, eggs benedict, champagne, flowers, and friends. A few days before the party, Kitty called and told Bob that the cook would not be able to attend. He said there was no problem, as he could make the eggs benedict dish, hollandaise sauce and all for the 60 invitees. Bob arrived Easter morning with a few cooking items and two long stem yellow roses, one for Kitty and one for Lili. They talked only a short time as the guests were arriving and the quartet began to play.

Bob socialized briefly with the arriving guests and then organized in the kitchen to prepare the brunch. As he began to make the hollandaise sauce, Ron, Lili's boyfriend, pitched in to cook the poachers, a welcomed offer. There was an instant bond between the two with laughter as they dove into preparation of the meal. Everyone was delighted with the outcome, especially Lili and Kitty. Compliments to the chefs!

Friends stayed on until late in the afternoon when suddenly, the house was empty. Bob looked at Kitty and asked, "Where did everyone go?" She simply smiled and replied, "They're gone."

They topped it off with dinner and a fun flying movie that Bob wanted to see with Kitty, *High Road to China*. They dated between Vail and Boulder for over a month when one morning Kitty got a phone call from Jim Okonek who was now the owner of K2 Aviation. He wanted her to come to Talkeetna to fly for K2 for the upcoming climbing and hunting season. He referred to Kitty as his chief pilot, but Kitty would say that was because she was his only other pilot! Kitty became very excited during the call. She was being offered the opportunity to fly for K2 and her C185, *Red Fox*, in the elements she was so fond of.

In her excitement, she explained this great opportunity to Bob. The relationship was just beginning and Bob was wondering, "What now?"

After a moment of silence that seemed an eternity, Kitty asked Bob if he would like to come to Talkeetna with her for the summer and work on getting his private pilot's license. Bob had started flying and soloed at age 16 but was not able to continue. His father, George, was a decorated captain and squadron leader in WWII, flying 52 missions in the South Pacific in a B-25 Mitchell. He had always wanted Bob to fly.

Being the off-season for Bob's job, he had the time and so began a new chapter for both of them.

Kitty was off to Alaska the next week to begin flying climbers to Mt. McKinley. Soon after, Bob joined her in Talkeetna with his dog, Ruby Begonia. He had not been back to Alaska since buying property on Katie Lake in 1969. Bob's introduction to Alaska bush flying was with Kitty on a run to the McWilliams Gold Mine to pick up core samples in the Cessna 185. Flying over dense forest and hilly terrain, Kitty pointed out their landing site in the distance, a spot that looked like a postage stamp in the trees in a box canyon.

As they got closer on final approach, Bob grabbed his camera and snapped a few pictures. The runway was a short, narrow, uphill dirt patch with a huge hump in the middle. They were descending quickly over treetops in order set down and use as much of the strip as possible.

With the wheel skis just clearing the trees, Kitty settled the beefy plane onto the dirt strip, but as they went over the hump, the plane bounced airborne briefly, ruining her perfect landing. "Damn hump!" Kitty mumbled on the head set.

With that, she got on the brakes and brought the plane to a stop, 75 feet from the end of the strip. She spun it around with a burst of power so it would be facing downhill for their departure. This was definitely a new experience for Bob.

Kitty hopped out and strode toward the cluster of cabins and a Quonset hut where the miners were. Mr. McWilliams lit up a smile when he saw her and immediately made a spot for her to sit down with him and the mining crew at a big table for a cup of coffee. After chatting over coffee, they headed out to shuttle several heavy bundles of core to the plane and loading them per Kitty's direction for placement in the 185. Bob wondered if the plane would be able to get airborne with the added weight.

Kitty was used to this routine. Once loaded up, the two climbed aboard and she said, "Ready?" She fired up, stood on the brakes for the short field takeoff, brought the power in, and the big 300-horsepower engine roared. She released the brakes and started down the rutted dirt strip. They hit the hump and the plane tried to fly, settled a bit then struggled to gain speed and altitude. Kitty eased back on the yoke and they cleared the tree tops with not much to spare as they headed back to Talkeetna. Kitty says, "He passed his first test."

Kitty was busy flying climbers to Denali in the Cessna 185 and delivering supplies and people to remote lakes in the floatplane during the day, and in the evening Alaskan light, she spent time teaching Bob to fly in an old Cessna 150. It had no starter so she had to hand prop start the engine each time. The right door latch was broken, so it would only stay closed in the steady slipstream. They flew together nearly every evening in the midnight sun for over six weeks of training while Kitty pushed Bob to learn flight maneuvers and develop landing skills. The evening hues of dimmed sunlight were unforgettable.

During the day, Mike Fisher was Bob's other instructor. Early in his training with Fisher, he was taught how to handle an engine out situation. Shortly after takeoff, Fisher pulled the power to idle and asked Bob where he was going to land.

Bob said, "Can't turn around to make the runway and no clear spot ahead!"

Fisher calmly said, "You see those two big trees with a space in the woods behind them? Set up to land between them, making sure you strike both wings on the trees at the same time and we will slip right through into that little clearing."

Bob was suddenly thinking, "Is this for real?"

He set the plane up for the crash, and just in time, Fisher pushed the engine power back up and they flew away barely above tree top, a lesson well imprinted. Bob never forgot to always be ready to pick the "best spot" to put down in case of an engine out situation.

While having breakfast at the Roadhouse with Kathy Sullivan one morning, Kathy mentioned to Kitty that she needed some help at her property on Pirate Lake. Her cabins needed some work. One was sinking in the mud and another had damage from a bear.

Kitty told her, "Take Bob to Pirate with you. He can help."

Somewhat skeptical, Kathy quizzed Bob on what he knew about fixing cabins in a remote location not far from the base of Denali. Mildly convinced he might be of some use, Kathy agreed to take him out to the lake. The next day, the two met to discuss the damage and needed repairs so Bob could figure out what supplies to bring. The list included a two-ton auto jack, a soldering torch, and appropriate parts for fixing a destroyed gas copper tubing gas line to a stove, along with other assorted items.

Kitty loaded the C185 floatplane with the gear and food and got Kathy and Bob seated along with her friend, Dr. Peter Hackett, who was going along for the ride. Off they flew to Pirate Lake. Landing on the lake is from north or south, avoiding both swamp and rocks. They touched down on the glassy water and taxied to a clearing where the rustic little Tokosha Cabin sat where they unloaded the equipment.

As Kitty fired up the 185 to taxi out, she said, "See you in a couple of days."

Pirate Lake is where Kathy felt most at home. She lived there for years, gave birth there, and was comfortable to be back at the cabins.

As it was a warm day, Kathy turned to Bob and asked, "Do you mind if I take my shirt off?"

Bob, surprised at the request, answered, "No, not at all."

Kathy tossed her shirt onto a blueberry bush. Kitty made the turn and headed the floatplane down the lake for takeoff. As the plane picked up speed, Kitty glanced at the two standing on the bank, Kathy topless and waving.

The plane lifted off the short lake and climbed out over the trees, and as the sound droned off, Kathy said, "Do you mind if I take my pants off? I like to work without heavy clothing on and we've got work to do."

Again, Bob replied, "No problem."

So, there in the wilderness was this six-foot tall, beautiful girl in a pair of pink underwear with hip boots on. In deference to the location, she did keep Genet's 44-Magnum pistol strapped around her waist as they headed through the low brush to the first cabin needing repair.

Kathy explained, "We are going to work on the Ruth Cabin first. The bear ripped the door off the leather hinges, entered the cabin, and tore the propane gas stove off the wall."

Bob was thinking, "Hope the bear is at someone else's cabin."

In fact, the bear had pretty much shredded the cabin. Trying to look Kathy in the eyes as she outlined the damage, Bob assessed where to start and went to work while Kathy straightened things up.

Not long after, she asked him with a little laugh, "How did you do that so fast?"

Bob replied, "Wasn't too bad. What's next?"

They headed to the Alouette Cabin, which on one corner had sunken a foot or so into the soggy tundra.

"Think we can fix this one?" Kathy asked.

Bob replied, "Well, we'll jack it up, dig the holes deeper for the pylons, fill the holes with rocks, and set the cabin back on the adjusted pylons."

Bob told Kathy that they'd need lots of good size rocks, so they walked the short distance to the lake and peered into the crystal-clear water. The rocks they would need were close to shore but getting wet would be necessary. Laughing, they agreed that Bob would get muddy under the cabin and Kathy would get wet moving rocks. After jacking the corner up and stabilizing it, Bob began digging out the pylons in the tight area under the cabin while Kathy was bringing rocks up from the lake. Out of the blue, Bob heard loud splashing followed by a string of cussing.

"Everything OK, Kathy?" Bob shouted sarcastically.

Kathy burst into laughter after slipping into the water and yelled back, "Yes, all fine."

Still in her "work outfit," soaking wet, and still laughing, she continued hauling large rocks up to the cabin.

Bob peered out from his mucky hole and asked, "That all you can carry?"

They both broke into laughter at the whole situation. Several hours later, three of the support pylons had been reset and the cabin rested level and solid in its new position. Back at the Tokosha Cabin, evening came and Kathy produced a wonderful wilderness dinner as they sat at the campfire getting to know each other while admiring the spectacular view of Denali in the evening light. It was time to hit the sack after a long, funny day.

As they entered the little cabin, Bob noticed two small bunks. The upper had lots of supplies and equipment on it and Kathy casually said, "We can both sleep in the bottom bunk. Kitty wouldn't mind, we're good friends." Then she added, "We can sleep head to toe."

Bob thought, "Wow, every man's dream. Pretty girl, small bed in this spectacular wilderness . . ."

They then agreed to clear off the upper bunk for Bob and climbed in with a back and forth "good night." Bob dozed off, his mind reviewing one of the most interesting days of his life.

The next day the two worked on the other cabins. Kitty was supposed to come to pick them up but the weather was not cooperating, so she could not fly into the lake. Kathy and Bob had another fun, productive day and great evening meal by the fire as Denali appeared and they spent another quiet night in the cozy cabin.

Kitty arrived the next morning in beautiful sunshine. They loaded the floatplane and headed back to Talkeetna; mission accomplished. The two women got together at the Roadhouse for coffee to catch up on the trip into Pirate Lake. Kathy, in a fun mood, told Kitty the whole story, all parts, and they had a good laugh. She said that Bob was so funny and that she was impressed with his ability to figure out and fix anything with limited supplies.

Kathy had, by then, lost her partner, Ray Genet, to a climbing accident on Mt. Everest. She had gone to Pirate Lake with Bob and returned with a renewed view that some men could, maybe, keep up with her. Kitty and Bob laughed and agreed that Kathy was a very special person and friend to Kitty and was willing to share *anything*. Kitty thought he surely passed his second test.

Bob continued flight training with Kitty and Mike throughout the summer. Days involved cross-county flying along the glaciers and landing on gravel riverbeds. He received his private pilot certificate in Alaska before returning to Colorado with his dog, Ruby. A third test passed with flying colors.

The 1983 season with K2 was busy with lots of flying for Kitty on both skis and floats. Along with many trips to the McWilliams mine with supplies, air drops to miners on the "high road," and flying core samples out of the gravel bar on the river, she flew a wonderful man, Willie Burkhardt. He and his assistant came from Switzerland to photograph Denali and the Alaska Range. She flew them at the same times each day, early morning and late evening, for four hours a day to get similar lighting and distance from the mountain. Although they did not speak fluent English, they communicated with gestures and smiles. The aerial photographs were pieced together with many horizontal frames to make a beautiful, long mountain poster printed in Switzerland.

One morning, Kitty received a call from Julie Okonek. She was concerned about her son, Brian Okonek, who was guiding an Italian expedition in the Little Switzerland area. They were ten days overdue for their pickup time. Concerned about their safety and lack of food provisions, she felt that they had decided to leave the landing area on the Pika Glacier. Pika was a small glacier off the Kahiltna Glacier with world class rock climbing. The walk out route was difficult and dangerous in stormy weather. Jim had tried multiple times to evacuate the climbers but, with bad weather, was unable. Kitty said that she would give it a go since Jim was busy on another flight. She went to the Park Service Station to ask Roger Robinson, a ranger and climber, to come along as he knew the walk-out route. He figured they might hike the Pika Glacier to Exit Pass then on to the Granite Glacier to Wildhorse Pass, which would take them to the Tokositna River. From there they could catch a riverboat ride to Talkeetna.

Robinson was a bit apprehensive about flying into the spooky and ominous canyon. Kitty didn't like it either and turned back to fly up the terminal moraine of the Kahiltna Glacier. They circled several times, peeking down through clouds that obscured the Pika. They finally saw a break in the clouds and sighted the climbers below. Kitty, sandwiched between the low clouds and the flat light of the glacier, set up for the glacier landing. After shutting down the engine, Roger jumped out to hugs and greetings from the excited and hungry Italians. To get his anxious clients out, Brian loaded them in the airplane and asked Roger to wait on the glacier with him until Kitty or Jim came back to pick them up along with the rest of the gear. Roger laughed, looking down at his lightweight uniform and gym shoes, and agreed to stay on the glacier with Brian until the next flight out. The weather slowly lifted and Jim made it back in time to fly out the rest of the party.

It was late August when Kitty flew five kayakers, Rob Lesser, John Wasson, Bo Shelby, John Markel and Chris Roach, into Stephan Lake to run the Talkeetna River. It was an exercise in external load management on the floatplane.

Jim Okonek & Kitty,
Talkeetna Alakasa, October, 2016

Kitty's Diary:

We tied and secured two skirted kayaks along each float, aft of the propeller and then I flew two round trips, with three guys and two kayaks on the first trip and two guys and three kayaks on the second. On the first flight with the two-kayak exterior load, the Cessna flew

along just above a stall. The second flight, we strapped on three kayaks with one in the middle of the spreader bars. I was amazed. The plane actually flew better with the third kayak in the middle, giving it more lift off the lake.

Jim Okonek, picnic on glacier

Lesser kayak party, Murder Lake, Rob Lesser photo

On another flight, Jim Okonek flew Wasson and Lesser to the Susitna, landing on the turbulent river while it was running at 33,000 cubic feet per second, (cfs). Okonek's upstream takeoffs were intense, Wasson and Lesser remembered. The water ran so fast, even they aborted their Devil's Canyon attempt at that time. On September 1, Kitty's birthday, she flew to High Lake, a narrow airstrip above Devil's Canyon, for a pick up where hydrologists were doing feasibility studies for the hydroelectric dam project.

Kitty's Diary:

Curt, Kim, & Rob,
Lesser kayak trip

The hydrologists wanted me to deliver a message that the river was running at a very high volume from all of the rain we've had over the summer and it was not advisable for the kayakers to try to attempt Devil's Canyon, an unrated whitewater that had never been successfully run and where a kayaker had died during an ABC film project the year before. I delivered the message of caution to Rob Lesser and the guys.

Sept 4ᵗʰ: Wasson, Shelby, and Lesser left with Okonek at 6:30 a.m. for the Devil's Canyon run. They flew to a lake by Stephan, but closer to the canyon. At the same time, Markel and Roach flew onto the river with Cliff Hudson. I flew three videographers to the muddy High Lake airstrip to film the kayakers coming down the run.

Unloading kayak

After flying a couple of hunting trips, I flew back and picked up the photographers at the High Lake airstrip. It was a beautiful flight back with Kim "Kimosabe" Leatham buzzing the successful Devil's Canyon kayakers on the Susitna River. We all had a potluck dinner at K2 to celebrate!

Floatplane at High Lake

The next night with the Devil's Canyon boy's back in town, they showed video river run films at Nancy and Mac's Latitude 62.

With the season drawing to a close in November, Kitty flew south to Vail, Colorado, where Bob was in the process of purchasing a 1968 Cessna 182 *N42849* out of Glenwood Springs. It had been well-cared for and flew beautifully. After Kitty helped Bob get acquainted with the plane in the tricky crosswinds at the Eagle County Airport, where they based the C182, they flew often to Aspen and to other mountain airstrips.

In the spring of 1984, Bob flew his airplane to Three Lakes, Wisconsin, to meet up with Kitty at the Banner family summer home. Together, they headed to Woolrich, Pennsylvania, where Kitty had an interview with the Woolrich Company to possibly be the "Woolrich Gal" for their new ad program. They then flew on to Connecticut, where Bob had a company meeting to attend.

Kitty took advantage of being on the East coast to fly to Martha's Vineyard to visit her friend, Carolyn Cullen and landed on the little airstrip at Oak Bluffs Airport where she had worked in 1976. It was great reconnecting with Carolyn and Val. Kitty was asked to fly a couple of the Edgartown Yacht Club Regatta racing champs to Newport, Rhode Island, where she experienced marine fog in high density traffic on her flight back to Connecticut to reconnect with Bob. There, they parked the airplane and headed off for Europe. While Bob was ski testing for Olin on the glaciers in Solden, Austria, Kitty was fitted with a new pair of locally-made hiking boots. She took advantage of the spectacular high alpine trails with

236

breathtaking panoramic views and mountain huts that served delicious strudel and schnapps. It was like out of a movie. As she would round a corner after hiking to the top, there would be men playing accordions in their traditional feathered hiking hats and lederhosen merrily singing and swinging their mugs of draught beer.

When the test was finished, they traveled to Innsbruck, Venice, and Monte Carlo, where they swam in the warm Mediterranean. They hiked in the mountains of Chamonix and Zermatt beneath the Matterhorn, where Bob ran a ski race camp for several years. Europe was home to so many of the climbers that Kitty had flown in Alaska.

Upon their return, they flew the Cessna to Bridgeton, Maine, to visit Bob's family. From there it was on to Stowe, Vermont, where Kitty did a photo shoot ad for North Face with Jan Reynolds and Ned Gillett entitled *Behind every woman is North Face*. After the photo shoot, they pointed the plane westward.

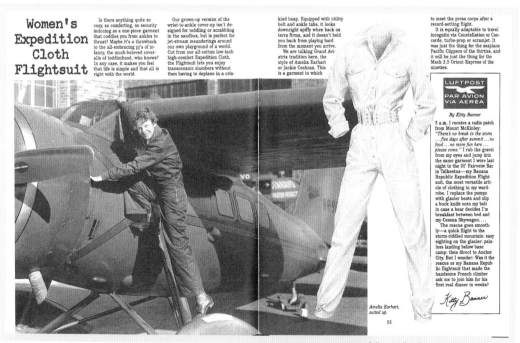

Banana Republic Flightsuit, 1986

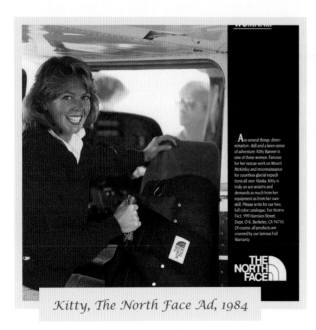

Kitty, The North Face Ad, 1984

On June 15, 1985, surrounded by family and friends, Kitty and Bob married in the Vail Interfaith Chapel. With the Rocky Mountains as a backdrop on a blue bird day, they danced and partied in Vail. It snowed the next morning, and the morning after that. Despite a United Airlines labor strike, they managed to make it to Maui to enjoy a much-needed rest.

Within a week of returning to Colorado, Kitty flew to Anchorage to begin work in Talkeetna on the Sir Edmund Hillary documentary film project with Jim Shaw, Aspen Film Ranch, which aired on the Discovery Channel. For the project, she was contracted to be folk singer John Denver's flight instructor for his seaplane rating in the film.

For years, Kitty and Steve "General" Sheridan, a good friend of Bob's and part-owner of Performance Sports Ski Shop in Vail, had been pushing Bob to build a log cabin on his piece of land on Katie Lake, accessible only by floatplane. Bob and Steve flew to Anchorage and were picked up at Lake Hood by Jim Okonek, who flew

*Kitty & Bob's wedding
invitation photo, 1985*

them to Talkeetna. While Kitty was getting ready for the filming project, Bob and Steve began to arrange their gear for the trip into Katie Lake. One hundred trees had to be cut down, limbed, and stripped of bark to dry for construction of the cabin the following year. Bob hired three young guys traveling through Talkeetna to help with the work. Kitty flew several loaded trips into the lake with the guys and gear. Finding the boundary corners of the property took some doing in the heavy underbrush. They set up camp in a little clearing where the cabin would be built overlooking Katie Lake. They worked four twelve-hour days to get the work accomplished.

Meanwhile, Kitty was busy with the film project. John Denver arrived from Aspen, Colorado, in his distinctively painted Cessna 210, buzzing the runway to announce his arrival before landing. As he got out of the plane, he loudly exclaimed "Talkeetna!" with his signature smile.

Guitar and gear in hand and with a film crew from the Aspen Film Ranch Production Company, he headed straight to the floatplane dock. Kitty met John on the dock. They were joined by Jim Bailey, manager of the Stephan Lake Lodge, who flew in with his Cub. Denver told her that it was his dream for many years to learn to fly floats in Alaska. After an in-depth briefing, Kitty carefully stood on the float and manually hand-prop started the engine from behind. Climbing into the back seat, she then gave John the controls, along with instructions to follow, as they taxied to the end of the lake for the water takeoff from Christiansen Lake en route to Stephan Lake Lodge.

JOHN DENVER
ASPEN FILM RANCH DOCUMENTARY - 1985

Needing a bit of on-site help at the lodge, Kitty invited Kathy Sullivan to join her with the crew. That evening after air-to-air filming, dinner, and John serenading with his guitar, it was suggested that they all take a sauna. Kitty, choosing to review her flight lessons for the next day, declined. When the generator lights went out at 8:00 p.m., she lit a candle to continue studying. Kathy returned to the room she was sharing with Kitty. With a big grin Kathy asked if John could spend the night with them. She felt "he might be lonely, alone in his room." Thinking she was kidding, Kitty said yes. Kathy left the room, and shortly after, Kitty heard some rumbling coming down the hall and was surprised as Kathy entered the room holding one end of his mattress under her arm. Then John, in his pajamas, appeared holding the other. They placed the mattress, sheets, pillow and blanket on the floor between the log beds. Kathy climbed into her bed and John settled into his new accommodations on the floor.

John Denver, Doug, & locals,
with Bob & Kitty on left,
Fairview Celebration,
Mike Vaughn photo

Laughing, Kitty said, "Good night, Kathy. Good night, John."

Kathy added, "Good night, Kitty. Good night, John."

John responded with, "Good night, Kitty. Good night, Kathy. Good night, John boy."

They all laughed themselves to sleep. Kitty often jokes that she slept with John Denver on her honeymoon. Back at the Fairview Bar we all celebrated John's seaplane rating and the Aspen Film Ranch documentary.

In the spring of 1986, Doug Geeting, owner of Geeting Aviation, called Kitty. He asked her to come to Talkeetna to fly for him for the upcoming climbing season. Excitedly, she accepted the offer. She told Doug that Bob would also be coming up with a crew for the construction of their cabin at Katie Lake.

Doug Geeting in Pitts Special

Soon after the call, Kitty was northbound. She had contacted her friend, Ralph Wing, an award-winning Alaskan log cabin builder. He agreed to head-up the project using the trees cut the prior year.

Bob and Steve gathered a group of ski racers Bob had coached at Ski Club Vail in the 1970s with Mike, Jay, Jonathan, Todd and Gaylynn. They, along with other friends, headed north from Colorado to build the cabin. In three vehicles loaded with supplies, chain saws, beer and multiple sleeves of Copenhagen, they journeyed up the Alaskan Highway to Talkeetna.

Kitty arranged for Boyd Gochanour with his Susitna Air Turbo Cessna 206 on floats to fly in the dimensional lumber for the flooring, roof structure, metal roofing, wood stove, chainsaws, food, building materials and even the kitchen sink. It took more than 16 trips in the powerful Cessna 206 to get all the construction materials on site. On one trip in, Boyd told the crew to unload quickly. He'd struck a rock while landing on a river and had punched a hole in one of the floats. As he taxied out onto the lake, the float was mostly submerged, but he punched the power and took off successfully with water spewing like a fire hose from the float.

While Kitty was flying climbers and float trips for Geeting, she worked in over 70 Super Cub runs to the lake with supplies, food, and assorted guests, to help with the construction. Hearing that the ridge log for the roof was scheduled to be put into place, Kitty and Kate Sheldon decided to fly in for a roof raising party. Kate raided her closet and found her floor-length, gold lame' prom dress and grabbed her sister Holly's off-the-shoulder long, white lace dress for Kitty. They filled a basket with blueberries, pastries,

Kate Sheldon & Kitty, roof raising party
Katie Lake Cabin, 1986

244

chocolates, and of course, Cook's "Champagne," and headed for the floatplane at Christiansen Lake. Kitty, dressed in lace, installed the battery, hopped in, fired the engine, and flew low-level up the Talkeetna River to Katie Lake. The cabin-building crew was surprised and excited to drop their chainsaws and celebrate in the midnight sun.

Kitty's Diary:

We had flown in a kitchen sink and it was time to dig a well. At only eight feet down they hit the most incredible crystal-clear water any of us had ever tasted. With four to five feet of rock in the hole, they ran a black pipe to the pitcher pump at the kitchen sink. A Paloma water heater was included in the plumbing with the showerhead placed on the outside of the building and a stone pad to stand on.

Kitty, Bob, & Ruby Begonia, Katie Lake Cabin

While being totally exposed to the woods behind the cabin, and all soaped up, you could catch sight of a moose walking on the game trail just about 80 feet from where you were showering. Todd Brown and Mike

Bob, Mike, Ralph, Jonathan, Todd, General Sheridan, Jay, & Gaylynn on Katie Lake

Mooney dug and built the outhouse about 60 feet from the cabin. One had to be vigilant prior to their run to the outhouse on the path through the blueberry bushes, a favorite snack of the local black bears. Gaylynn, affectionately called the "camp wench," Mike Mooney's gal, along with Jonathan were a strong part of the crew.

Bob made the interior stairs to the loft with one 16-inch round birch log, propped up to the loft at a 45-degree angle, with notches for each two-foot quarter round stair and glued and spiked into the notch.

Bob, fishing, Katie Lake

Mike Brown, a U.S. Team World Cup ski racer, Colin Gleeson, both from Vail, and John Mouw, now from Homer, were among the first "guests" to help. Mike built a beautiful rock shield on the log cabin wall behind the wood stove. The 10/12 *pitch roof was finished with a Denali blue metal roof and was easily seen when flying over the cabin. Five weeks from start to finish.*

On July 2nd, we had a fly-in barbeque cabin party. Roberta and Kate Sheldon, Don Lee, Sheridan, Jay and Jonathan, Nancy, Kathy and Adrian and a few others flew in for the party. Don Lee picked up the chainsaw and carved a bear head, complete with a lit cigarette, on one of the stumps near the cabin.

Bob & Kitty, First Spike, Katie Lake Cabin

Kitty flew most of the crew out of Katie Lake. Sheridan, Jonathan, and Jay trekked through the rugged Devil's Club tundra for two hours with the raft on their shoulders to the Talkeetna River. When they got to the low brush near the river they surprised a grizzly. It was like *Keystone Cops*. Jonathan, at the front of their cargo, jerked backwards, causing Jay, carrying the 44 Magnum, to be pinned beneath the raft and supplies. Sheridan grabbed for the gun while the bear stood up

Katie Lake Cabin Crew

247

tall, clacking its teeth at the shocked threesome. The bear apparently decided that they were not worth eating, or maybe he could count and felt outnumbered. Nevertheless, it took off, loping away before a shot could be fired. When they got closer to the riverbank, Sheridan fell into a bear den that was hidden by six-foot fiddlehead ferns. As fast as they could, they put the raft together and launched for the float to Talkeetna. Shortly after, they spotted Kitty and Bob flying overhead as they buzzed the "three men in a tub" floating down the river while passing around a bottle of whiskey. They made it to Talkeetna just in time for the festive 4th of July celebration, fireworks and all.

Weeks later, on their first wedding anniversary, Kitty flew Bob, and Ruby Begonia into Katie Lake to varnish the floor inside and empty the food and furniture, wrap it, and set it in boxes out on the deck. Waiting for the varnish to dry, they jumped into the Super Cub and took off for Papa Bear Lake to check on a well the crew had dug for Doug Geeting's cabin. Bob forgot to bring the generator cable and the gun so Kitty flew back to get both. She returned with the cable, but forgot the gun. When finished, the three flew back to Katie Lake. As they touched down, Bob looked out and thought he saw a bear. Now Bob had been accused of having "bear-anoia"

Sheldon Family on Ruth Glacier

while building the cabin and was nicknamed "Bear Bait Bob Banner." He was vigilant about keeping a clean camp and kept the food supply in a tent away from the crew. Ironically or intentionally, the guest tent was next to the food tent.

Kitty taxied to the dock and as Bob was tying the plane up. Ruby and Kitty raced up the hill to find the supplies and food scattered everywhere. She and Ruby froze.

Bob arrived, and in the mess, noticed a leaking honey bear container with puncture holes. He bolted into the cabin, grabbed the gun, ran around the corner, and came face-to-face with the bear. Ruby started to charge, but when the six-foot black bear stood up, Ruby retreated quickly and hid behind Bob

Roberta at the Sheldon Mountain House

and Kitty. Bob took one shot over the bear's head to scare it away and it turned tail and ran.

After cleaning up the mess and moving everything back inside, they set up bear boards. Plywood sheets with nails driven through facing the intruder were placed on the deck and over the windows, creating an effective deterrent for a bear thinking the cabin housed an easy snack. With the cabin closed, they headed back to Talkeetna.

Sheldons at Sheldon Mountain House

Roberta Sheldon called Kitty one day and asked her to fly her family to the Don Sheldon Mountain House, built in 1966 in the Amphitheater on the Ruth Glacier. As Kitty was booked and flying all day, she suggested that maybe one of the other pilots could fly them up.

Roberta replied, "No, we'll wait. We want you to fly us."

Roberta and the kids finally met Kitty at the airport raring to go and dressed in big fur-clad collared parkas. Kitty loaded them into the Cessna 185. They were so excited, laughing and singing into the headphone mics that after the briefing, Kitty turned down the intercom radio volume so she could listen for transmissions. They flew up the braided river, spotting bear and moose along the way. It was a breathtaking flight up through the Great Ruth Gorge with its mile-high granite walls and intense blue turquoise melt water dotting the glacier. Along the way, they flew around Mt. Dickey and the Moose's Tooth, passed over the Ruth Ice Field, and finally turned for the approach to land on the 6,000-foot level of the Ruth Glacier.

Kitty's Diary:

After coming to a stop, we got out and I walked back to take a picture of the Sheldons by the red C185 on wheel skis. They asked me to count to three and on the count Holly and Kate opened up their parkas. They were wearing bikinis! Robert in his swim trunks right on cue, too!

We spent all evening up at The Mountain House, basking in the everlasting Alaskan sun. We had a picnic and snacked on fiddlehead ferns, freshly picked blueberries, and other treats while sitting on the dramatic rock outcropping above the cabin listening to Roberta's favorite Willie Nelson songs blasting on the boom box.

Turns out it was Kate and Robert's first memorable trip up to their dad's famed Mountain House, their first time there as a family. It was such a special time for all of us, and one of my most memorable and unforgettable flights. It was truly an honor to be invited into both their home and hearts.

"It was my last of many flights for the day, a scenic up to the Ruth Glacier. The Cessna 185 was loaded with 5 passengers from New York," Kitty recalled.

She had landed on a soot-soaked glacier, fallout from a volcanic eruption the past winter that blew over the Alaska Range. "The glacier was pitted from all the black ash, and it was late in the day, so the glacier was soft. We waited a while for it to harden for a firm takeoff," she remembered.

"While taking off and just at the point of rotation, as the plane began to fly, there was a loud bang from the tail," Kitty said. She felt a powerful shudder in the rudder pedals. "Before deciding to leave the glacier landing site, I wanted to make sure that the skis would fully retract for a landing back on the Talkeetna State Airport. I looked down at the left ski to confirm that it cycled back to wheel and asked my talkative passenger to confirm that the right ski had cycled as well. I explained that we'd bypass the ice fall and head straight to Talkeetna," she said.

Doug at Geeting Aviation town office, Talkeetna, Alaska

Kitty & Doug, navigation briefing, Fairview Bar

The unsuspecting passengers shot through rolls of film, threw snowballs at each other, and gazed at the tremendous vertical rise of granite jetting around them.

Guessing that it was a problem with the tail of the airplane, Kitty radioed Talkeetna Flight Service to request an advisory and they cleared the area of all aircraft so she could set down quickly. Little did she know that the tail wheel assembly had sheared off and was only attached by the rudder cables. It was flailing in the wind and causing the shuddering.

Doug & Kitty, Kahiltna Glacier

"I had planned to fly around the Don Sheldon Amphitheatre, the Ruth Ice Fall, and then over to the Moose's Tooth and Broken Tooth before heading back through the Great Gorge to Talkeetna," Kitty said.

Before takeoff, she rearranged the passengers seating so that the weight balance in the plane would be correct for the downhill run takeoff on the glacier. She directed the heaviest person to sit up front with her to balance most of the weight forward. The passengers put on their headsets, tuned in, and were waiting to hear Kitty's commentary on the passing mountains, wildlife, and lakes. One of the passengers, a talkative sort, sat right seat and barraged her with questions about flying, geology, and snow science.

Bob was in the Geeting Aviation office that day and heard Kitty's radio transmission. Concerned, he headed out to the strip to see Kitty come in. He saw the tail assembly dangling and flipping around as the Cessna 185 was on short final. Maintaining control on landing would be challenging. Kitty set up for a main-wheel touch down and then, keeping enough power to hold the tail up, slowed slightly to make the 90-degree turn to the air taxi office. She brought the tail down as easily as possible and skidded a short distance to a halt, still a noticeable distance from the flight office. She hopped out and began unloading the passengers. As they walked to the office, full of excitement, they thanked Kitty for a great flight, noticing the twisted tail assembly.

Doug & Kitty, briefing

Don Lee & Kitty,
Ruth Glacier

Kitty & Ruby, C185

Ruby ready for takeoff

"Our longtime ace mechanic, Harold 'the Wrench' Maness, came out to inspect the plane and said, 'Ah, this is the old Porter rig,'" she remembered.

The part was a temporary replacement while the stock assembly was in repair. The plane would not pass the 100-hour inspection due to all of the wear and tear from rough landing sites. Apparently, the Porter rig would not have passed either!

With Kitty's flying season at an end, a big thank you to Doug, and the cabin completed, Kitty, Bob, Steve and Ruby said goodbye to Talkeetna and their friends. They headed south in Steve's van down the 600 mile Cassiar Highway past huge glaciers, lakes and rivers to Prince Rupert, where they caught a ferry to Vancouver. They visited the incredible Vancouver World's Fair "Transportation," where the exhibits were filled with beautiful historic planes, trains and automobiles, along with the cultural history of natives in the Northwest. It had been quite an amazing Alaskan summer.

During the fall, Bob and Kitty flew their Cessna 182 often, visiting friends and providing aerial service for professional photographers and Channel 8 News in the Vail and Aspen area. That autumn, Kitty partnered with Bob as a manufacture sales representative in the ski industry. The newlyweds began a 28-year career in business together, representing Descente ski clothing, Peppers Eyewear and over 20 different brands. Often, in the ski shops throughout their sales territory of Colorado and Utah, they'd encounter climbing customers from Kitty's flying career in Alaska. Business in the territory grew and they became number one in North America for years with Descente ski apparel. Both were involved in product development and were instrumental in product design.

While running their company, Kitty and Bob raised Mick, now 28, and Corey, 26 instilling in them the love of adventure in flying and skiing.

K2 AVIATION 25TH ANNIVERSARY
1980 – 2005

Kimball & Kitty, K2 Founders

K2 AVIATION 25TH ANNIVERSARY
Continued

Mike, Don, Kimball, Kitty, & Ken

Mick & Corey on Ruth Glacier

Mick, Mike Fisher, & Corey

Mike Fisher & his new bike design

K2 AVIATION 25TH ANNIVERSARY
Continued

Kitty, Twigg, & Holly

Kathy, Kimball, & Kitty

Holly, Kitty, Kathy, & Kate

Kathy, Tony, & Kitty

Kimball with his C185

Kitty & Tony, Turbine Otter

Everyone in the family is a certified pilot and all often fly the family tandem seat taildragger, Scout.

In May 2005, with a spectacular view of Denali, Kitty Banner Seemann and Kimball Forrest, founders of K2 Aviation, marked the company's 25th anniversary with a flight to the Don Sheldon Amphitheater on the Ruth Glacier. K2 Aviation is now owned and operated by Suzanne and Todd Rust.

Kitty, Bob, and their boys flew to Anchorage to meet with Kimball and head to Talkeetna. With Kimball in his red Cessna 185, Bob, Mick and Corey flew from Anchorage. It was an incredible flight through a spectacular glacier canyon just off the water below and its towering ice walls. They were pumped when they landed in Talkeetna. Kitty, Kathy Sullivan Genet and Kate Sheldon drove up, stopping for food for their two-night stay at the Sheldon Mountain House. Roberta had graciously extended an invitation for all to be her guests on the mountain for the reunion.

After provisions were made, Kitty, Kate and Kathy flew up to the Ruth Glacier with Kimball in the Cessna 185. Bob and the boys flew with Tony Martin in K2's turbine Otter, compliments of Suzanne Rust, owner of K2. The next day they roped up and cross-country skied all around the glacier exploring crevasses, bergschrund and ice caves with climbing guide extraordinaire, Brian McCullough. Later in the day, another ski plane arrived with two young jet fighter pilots from Fairbanks who had been overseas and had just returned from duty. It was their first time to the Gorge and they said that "It was more frightening to land on the Ruth Glacier than it was to fly fighter missions." It was a great Alaskan night on the glacier with family, new friends and shared stories.

It was a wonderful celebration of 25 years of history for K2 Aviation at the Don Sheldon Mountain House - and nobody stepped off the cliff going to the outhouse!

Expedition gear to Ruth Glacier, 1978

Captain Michael Seemann

Corey Seemann, Jeff Cricco photo

Epilogue

Mick & Corey with Scout, Montana

Kitty and Bob have two sons, born and raised in Vail, Colorado. Michael "Mick" attended Montana State University in Bozeman, Montana, and graduated in May 2012 with a double major in Environmental Studies and Aviation. His pilot ratings include: Private, Commercial, Instrument, Seaplane, Certified Flight Instructor, Multi-Engine, Multi-Commercial & Instrument, and Airline Transport Pilot. He is currently flying as captain for Horizon Airlines based in Seattle, Washington, and living in Whitefish, Montana. Mick's interests, include flying the family American Champion Scout, skydiving, snow and water skiing, mountain and road bike riding, trials biking, kiteboarding, guitar, piano and cooking.

Corey graduated from Montana State University in December 2015 with a Bachelor of Arts degree. He is a professional extreme backcountry skier with numerous sponsors. Currently, Corey's pilot ratings include: Private, Commercial, Instrument, Seaplane, Multi-Engine, and Multi-Commercial & Instrument. He holds a Montana real estate brokers license. Corey's interests are skydiving, waterskiing, mountain and road bike riding, trials biking, hydroplane boating, kite boarding, drum playing, flying the family Scout, aerial photography, and cooking, specializing in artisan pizza. He is currently living in Whitefish, Montana.

In 2011, Kitty took Mick and Corey to Talkeetna to obtain their Alaskan backcountry tailwheel bush endorsements and seaplane ratings with Don Lee at his flight school, Alaska Floats and Skis. They had the opportunity to get together with Roberta Sheldon and several other good friends in Kitty's beloved "beautiful downtown Talkeetna."

Kitty and Bob retired from the ski industry in December 2012 and currently live in Three Lakes, Wisconsin, in the summer months, where they continue to share their love of lakes, forests and flying with their boys and close extended family. In the winters, they migrate to warmer weather in Los Barriles, Baja, Mexico, where they traded in their snow boots for flip-flops, kayaking, paddle boarding, biking, kite boarding and long morning walks on the beach. As often as they can, they return to the majestic Rockies and Alaskan Mountain Ranges.

On October 21, 2016, Kitty and Kimball were honored in Anchorage by the Alaska Air Carriers Association as Aviation Legends in the great state of Alaska and credited for starting K2 Aviation.

Aviation Legend Poster

*Banner Seemann Family
with Cub, Eagle, Colorado, 1995*

*Three Lakes, Wisconsin, 2015
Tony Vangalin photo*

Afterword

Tony Martin, K2 25th, Ruth Glacier

By Tony Martin
Brown Eyed Lady on the Mountain

There might be a thousand reasons why people come to Alaska. One of them should be to visit Mt. McKinley, Denali (The Great One). I was assigned to fly with Kitty, while she was working as an expediter for Houston Oil and Minerals out of an Anchorage office. On that clear cloudless day in May, the summit of the mountain was only a few air miles away. Its appearance was more than awesome as we began our final approach to land on the Kahiltna Glacier. If there should be a divine force in the universe, then it must go for inspiration, as humans do, to those glaciated ridges and ice fields.

The skis of the Cessna 185 touched down with a soft thud. The sound was no louder than the one made by the wheels of a large transport jet landing at La Guardia, New York. The rollout on the steep glacier airstrip was bumpy, but pleasantly uneventful. In a minute, the propeller stilled, and as the pilot began to crawl out of the aircraft, she was already giving commands on how to unload the enormous amount of cargo. Her name was Catherine Banner, or Kitty as she is known to those fortunate to know her.

The excitement of the climbers, who had already been delivered to the glacier and were awaiting the remainder of their gear, was electrifying. My own emotion was a tension akin to combat: the eyes became alert, the skin tingled, and the sense of anticipation grew keen. In a few moments, after the aircraft's departure, the climbers would be left alone to pursue their goals. Would they reach the summit? Yes! But, despite how eager and prepared they were, only if the Mountain Spirits allowed them to do so.

Our stay on the glacier was too short. Kitty had to return to Talkeetna for another flight. We waved to the three men and called: "Take care and good luck." With the expected requirements of the climb, it would be a month before they were ready to return to civilization. In minutes, our aircraft was pointed downhill for takeoff, and once again, we were airborne. My heart was rushing from the thrill, but for Kitty, it was routine. She was as much a professional pilot as she was a mountain flying daredevil.

On assignment before arriving in Talkeetna, the idea that anybody would pursue such a dangerous occupation had already caught my imagination. Was a person bold, fearless, or merely foolhardy for choosing a tiny aluminum aircraft and a monstrous mountain as his or her toy and playground? If a 20,310-foot mass of granite did not intimidate one, what, if anything, did?

Kitty found some time in her busy schedule to reply to some of my questions. Against the background of frontier Alaska, her answers proved to be delightful and illuminating. Kitty's interest in flying airplanes, initiated by her piloting brothers, was increased dramatically after taking flying lessons with an aerobatic air show professional and working at Carolyn Cullen's airstrip on Martha's Vineyard. She learned to fly in western

Washington State, and 'built' flying hours by island hopping across the San Juan Islands of Puget Sound and flying for Cullen over the Atlantic Ocean. She accumulated additional flight time cruising above the North American continent. Her travels took her from Southern Mexico to the Caribbean to Alaska, which she first visited in 1972. Today, Kitty is experienced on wheels, floats, and skis.

Kitty Banner Seemann's fledgling career was not all fun and roses. Like many beginning commercial pilots, Kitty paid her dues. She lived in an aircraft hangar and acquired much of her experience in taildraggers: a heavily laden 'rag-wing' Super Cub and the high-performance Cessna 185.

After Kitty's 1972 visit to Alaska, she returned in 1976 and challenged herself to tackle a job more commonly ascribed to male pilots--that of plying the skies of wild Alaska. This entailed mastering bush and glacier operations that other pilots generally admired, but many were loath to attempt. She threw herself into flying for Talkeetna Air Taxi until such time that, early in 1980 at the age of 28, she initiated and bought into a partnership with Kimball Forrest, a professional geologist, commercial pilot, and a very good friend. She and Kimball enthusiastically purchased Holland Air Service after an agreement was worked with Ken Holland in the Fairview Hotel. Holland was an experienced glacier driver and gregarious bush pilot who had operated his commercial flights out of Talkeetna and had carried a wide variety of customers throughout the Alaskan Range.

K2 is based on the first letters of their names, but also a name reminiscent of the massive mountain that is second only to Everest as the tallest mountain in the Himalayas. This title was crucial as an attraction for worldly mountain climbers familiar with the names of the highest elevations on each continent who sought the lofty goal of climbing each of the Seven Summits, one of which is Denali.

K2's bread and butter was earned in flying mountain climbers to the glaciers of Denali. Kitty admitted, "The climbers are an exciting bunch and very interesting people. Talkeetna turns into an international spa during climbing season. The satisfaction of my job comes from putting together people and flying, from being part of the expedition, and from the rapport between the climbers and the pilot. I enjoy getting clients to where they want to go."

Kitty's eyes brightened when she mentioned The Mountain. "It's spectacular," she said. "The scenery is fantastic. The weather, cloud patterns, and lighting are always changing. It's never the same. It's never tiresome. The pay isn't great but, it's the ultimate in single-engine flying."

Kitty breezed over her biggest scare, the whiteout dangers which are the hazards of high altitude flying. The time weather conditions chased her back up a canyon and she had to spend a night on a glacier, wondering if her aircraft's engine would start in the morning. She admitted, "So far, that has been my most exciting predicament."

Kitty responded to the question, "Do you want to climb the mountain?" with an emphatic, "Oh, yes! But, the climbing season is from April to July and that's our busy time. I don't know when I could do it."

The toughest of my inquiries that Kitty answered concerned her plans and goals. She did not answer quickly. "It's hard to say. I have none outside aviation. I'd like to get my flight instructor's certificate and, maybe later, a multiengine rating. I haven't thought about the airlines. As far as business is concerned, Kimball and I would like to expand by adding another aircraft diversifying so we can better utilize the geological interests."

Surprisingly, Kitty said she felt no competitive animosity as a female pilot in a male-dominated profession. "In Talkeetna, there is an abundance of cooperation within the flying community. In the air, everybody is helping each other." She smiled and added, "On the ground, business competition is fierce."

Trying to capture Kitty's motivations on paper was like trying to capture a swift peregrine falcon's diving flight on film. The picture was elusive and intoxicating. Suddenly, our brief conversation was over. Kitty's busy schedule and concern for her clients demanded that she return to work. Her parting comment was a request assurance that my enthusiastic opinions about her abilities and achievements would be toned down.

She said, "I'm not at all like the high pressure or high-power executive women I've read about in the lower 48. I just like doing what I'm doing."

She was convincing and her modesty was unfeigned. Would it be incorrect to compare her to another pioneer aviatrix, Amelia Earhart, who flew 'Just for the Fun of It?' Are there any other women in the world who make their livings flying on and off glaciers? But, should a woman be praised only because she flies against what she calls 'the fickle fates and the winds of Denali?' Perhaps not, but in its most intense moments, piloting an airplane, like climbing a mountain, can be reduced to not only a test of wits between brain power and nature, but also to a contest between self and circumstances. Regardless of gender, aviators and mountain climbers alike have the opportunity to push themselves into the unknown. And that in itself may be the unseen heroic quality deserving of notice.

Talkeetna, the sleepy little village of 300 people where Kitty and Kimball's business, K2 Aviation, was located, was one other highlight of the assignment. Translated from the Native Indian tongue, Talkeetna means 'plenty of water.' Situated 80 air miles north of Anchorage at the junction of the Talkeetna, the Chulitna, the "Big Su," and the Susitna Rivers, the village seemed to be one of those rare places where magic exists. There was that much friendliness, charm and romance to the area. Principally, the town's airstrips have been cast in the role of launching sites for the mountain climbers who come from all over the world to test and challenge their skills in the rugged terrain of the Alaskan Range. For years, Talkeetna has also been a gathering spot for hunters, trappers, hikers, fishermen, miners, river boaters and railroad men. The frontier spirit continues to be alive, well and kicking.

The people who live in Talkeetna proved to be as varied as storybook characters. It may even be possible to meet a majority of them in one night for a wild game potluck dinner in the crowded hallways of the Fairview Hotel on Main Street. If Jack London or Robert Service were to step out and say hello, a visitor would not be surprised. The duo would obviously belong in the mélange.

The Fairview Bar has, in some respects, been made into a shrine to two men: pilot Don Sheldon and guide Ray Genet. Respectively, each helped pioneer glacier landings and mountain climbing in the Alaska Range. Their portraits have been placed on the mantle of the bar room piano. On any given Saturday night, a male pilot who has inherited Don Sheldon's role as "King of the Mountain" might have been swapping stories and advice with Kitty, who may be considered the "Mountain's Princess!"

Although a person does not go North seeking a celebrity status, if that by chance happens, it is because the region, like the 19th century United States of America, can give rise to its own natural aristocracy. That part of the world has remained one, which belongs to those who are willing to give action to their dreams.

Before departing Talkeetna, in a moment of solitude, looking across the Susitna River at the Alaska Range which contains some of the last grand adventures left on earth, this writer could not help but get a feeling that might occur only once in a lifetime. It was a lyrical sensation that might make both small children and adults drop their mouths open in wonder and awe to dream the dream of explorers and pioneers whose creed has been to see and to do those things which have not been seen or done before.

In part, the original quest of the assignment was fulfilled. It was easy to see why any individual of high spirit, like Kitty, just a brown-eyed lady who flies on the mountain, would be attracted to those peaks and valleys. The land is royally spectacular. It could demand tribute from the best of its subjects.

In retrospect, Alaska highlights and thrives with human contradictions. Kitty, born in Chicago, was living comfortably in a log house without running water or electrical appliances. She held an inter-disciplinary degree in aviation and literature, yet she would unhesitatingly help Kimball change the airplane's oil or pump gas from a 55-gallon drum. And the sight of the Great Amphitheater of the Ruth Glacier more than supported her claim that 'living in rural Alaska is pretty damned exciting.'

It was surrealistic during that visit to listen to a haunting Irish ballad inside a log structure serving as K2's operational headquarters and to listen to the dialogue. In a scene that equally belonged in the Swiss Alps, Kitty and Kimball were discussing, deliberately and logically, the location of crevasses, all exceedingly difficult to see and each capable of swallowing an airplane whole. Sharing matter-of-fact glances, they seemed to acknowledge, "These are some of the hazards with which we must deal. They are as much a part of the job as are the splendors of natural beauty. We accept the terms of the double-edged sword."

The expressions belonged to two young people who possessed the admirable combination of self-confidence and poise without the added harshness of vanity. Perhaps no one can enter those mountains and leave without being transformed by their good measure.

And, friend, in passing by this area, be careful that the high ragged ridges of the Alaska Range do not steal your heart. Because one day, far away, you will discover that you have been commanded to return. And your soul, restless, will be urging you not to delay.

June 1981
The Alaska Airlines Complimentary Magazine

One Dollar

alaska fest

alaska fest

JUNE 1981

FEATURES

24 **The Wings of Her Dreams** By Galen Rowell
Kitty Banner is a partner in a flying service at Talkeetna, Alaska, whose main job is flying people onto mountains and glaciers.

Kitty on the Alaska Airlines Magazine cover, 1981

The Wings of Her Dreams

BY GALEN ROWELL

NTIL JANUARY 3, 1959, the cowboy was part of the pioneer heritage of all the western states. On that day in 1959 Alaska joined the union and made the exception. Horse and rider never left much of a mark on the Last Frontier, with its long arctic winters, thick boreal forest, and soggy summer tundra. Over vast expanses of the state "you can't drive, you can't walk, you can't swim." So by default, Alaska's would-be cowboys took to the air.

Bush pilots rate high among the folk heroes of this young land. Jay Hammond, the present governor, was a professional bush pilot for 28 years. When a feature story depicted the lives of 13 legendary Alaskan pilots, 10 were already dead in the saddle. The image of the bush pilot, as described by one of them, is as singular as that of the mountain men of old: "He's dirty, he has a ratty airplane, and he's alive. It's a myth, the bush pilot thing."

A green-eyed Irish lass from Chicago is an obvious exception. Kitty Banner isn't male, she isn't dirty, and her single-engined Cessna 185 is in mint condition. She is one of a handful of pilots in the world who make a profession of glacier landing and mountain flying. Her airplane is equipped with retractable skis, and the bulk of her business is transporting mountaineers and sightseers onto the glaciers surrounding 20,320-foot Mount McKinley, North America's highest peak. She owns and operates K2 Aviation with her partner, Kimball Forrest, in the one-street town of Talkeetna, Alaska.

An earlier Talkeetna pilot became world-famous during a bush-flying career that spanned four decades. Don Sheldon focused heavily on glacier flights, and he saved many lives. He did it not only through skill and innovation, but also by a special flair for grace under pressure. When he died a natural death in 1976, he

Galen Rowell is a mountaineer, a writer, and a photographer who is widely published. This month he's climbing in China. Kitty Banner's firm is K2 Aviation, Box 290, Talkeetna, AK 99676.

was buried within sight of the mountain with the epitaph, "He wagered with the wind and won."

Banner is quick to avoid comparison to Sheldon. "He was a unique man who deserved his legend. I'm just another bush pilot. I'm not trying to fill his shoes." Her destiny, however, had an important link to Sheldon's. After his death his air taxi certificate, which is a transferable commercial permit something like a liquor license, was bought by Jim Sharp of Colorado. Banner happened to be working at the Boulder airport driving a fuel truck when Sharp flew in with his bush plane. They talked about Alaskan flying and Sharp eventually offered her a job. Later that same year she went to Alaska to work for him at Talkeetna Air Taxi.

Cinderella similarities end there. Banner was not waiting for Prince Charming to rescue her from a lesser existence. She already had strong qualifications for Alaskan flying which she had developed entirely on her own. She kept a low profile and was not motivated, as Amelia Earhart was, by a craving to become a public figure through flying. Her craving was simply to do bush flying in Alaska, and she was seeking the right opportunity. She came from a close-knit Chicago family in which six out of eight immediate members fly, and even though one of her flying brothers is in the publishing business, her career has been devoid of media coverage.

As a child on flights with the same brother, her interest first lay outside the airplane. She loved to watch the clouds and look at a face of the earth so different from what she had seen from the ground or from the great height of a commercial jet. As she learned to fly, the esthetics of flight became as important as the basic functions. She discovered the inner world of flight, the deep human experience described so vividly in the writings of Antoine de Saint-Exupery; *discovered* because the words that have introduced millions of nonflying people to the thought world of the pilot brought flashes of recognition to her. Although she had no plans to fol-

low his course of action, she once came close to repeating one of Saint-Exupery's classic journeys across North Africa in a small plane. Although Banner's journey never took place, the story closely parallels that of her first job offer in Alaska and eventual purchase of an air service.

She and Kimball Forrest worked together at the Bellingham airport in Washington while they were students at the university there. A plane flew in from California bound for Ethiopia, where a war was being fought. It was a Cessna 185 (like the one she and Forrest now own in Alaska) and two pilots were flying it by way of Chicago, Newfoundland, Ireland, and Greece. Banner asked them, "How about if we go with you and help out with the Ethiopian flying?" After serious discussions, they were turned down for lack of credentials. At dawn the Cessna was on the runway ready for takeoff. Just like in the movies, a dramatic sunrise formed a backdrop and Banner and Forrest were running across the tarmac with sleeping bags in hand. "How about if we come along just for the ride?"

The pilot smiled, "I'd like to do that, but with two extra gas tanks in the back seat it would be a little cramped!"

Kitty Banner's flight instructor in Bellingham was a character Saint-Exupery might have created. David Rahm, a professor of geomorphology, used his spare time to tour the country as a stunt pilot. He owned a Bucker-Jüngmann biplane that had originally been a Luftwaffe trainer, and he also had a "bushy" Cessna 180. Seemingly diverse aspects of his life were integrated into an enriching whole. His pilot's view of landforms became a book, "Reading the Rocks of the Southwest." Like Saint-Exupery, Rahm had learned that "the machine which at first blush seems a means of isolating man from the great problems of nature, actually plunges him more deeply into them.... His essential problems are set him by the mountain, the sea, and the

Kitty Banner flies her Cessna 185 out of Talkeetna, mainly on mountain trips.

wind."

Banner, too, sought involvement with these natural elements both in and out of aviation. She had skied the mountains of Colorado, swum competitively, sky-dived, and water-skied. As with Rahm, she wanted a life in which aviation was but part of a greater whole, and she did not want any of the majors offered at the university. She persisted until the administration accepted her own proposed course of study for an interdisciplinary degree. She mixed such subjects as geology, geomorphology, climatology, and aerial photography with aviation to help her understand the earth from the air.

At the end of a semester not long before she graduated, she stuffed her possessions — bicycle, plants, and all — into the back of her Datsun pickup and left for her family's summer home in northern Wisconsin. She stopped in Athol, Idaho, where Rahm was to be giving an air show. Afterwards, Rahm invited her to fly all the way to Wisconsin with him in his open-cockpit biplane. Banner wondered what to do with her truck, so she approached a hefty 16-year-old farm boy on the field. "How would you like to drive to Wisconsin if I pay your expenses?" He ran home and brought back his mother. The boy had never been out of Idaho; his mother approved of the chance for him to travel.

The two machines set off at the same time; each had roughly the same speed. In the old Luftwaffe trainer, Banner and Rahm sat in tandem wearing helmet and goggles, unable to hear each other yell. As they crossed interesting landforms, Rahm scrawled notes and they passed them back and forth as an occasional pen flew off into the wind. Sometimes Rahm would turn on the plane's smoke system (installed for air shows) and do loops and rolls, creating designs in the sky.

The fun ended abruptly in a Midwest electrical storm. Banner had her sleeping bag tucked around her to keep her warm, as lightning crackled so near that an old barnstormer might have lit his cigarette off the plane's bolt heads. They managed to land in a grass field and wait out the storm. They arrived in Hale's Corner, Wisconsin, just as the farm boy pulled up in her truck with the imprint of a road sign on one of the Datsun's fenders. His adventure had been no less grand than theirs.

After graduation from college, Banner worked at an all-women's airfield on the island of Martha's Vineyard, off the coast of Massachusetts. It was operated by Carolyn Cullen, a spirited, ageless little woman who was a charter member of the "Ninety-nines," an organization formed by precisely that number of early women

pilots with Amelia Earhart as president. Earhart had stopped at the Vineyard to say goodbye to Cullen on her first trans-Atlantic flight, and Cullen still treasures the leather jacket she left behind on that visit.

Cullen disliked shoes. She flew barefoot, and she made Banner do likewise "to feel the pedals and find the vibrations." Esthetics were of prime importance to this Renaissance-woman aviator, who did her own mechanical work and could talk engineering in the same breath as women's rights. She would say, "You're good, Kitty, but you're going to be *even better*." She believed that women had to be more than the equal of men to be happy in male-dominated fields such as

"To have that woman land you on a glacier and fly off alone…"

aviation. She repeatedly said, "I'm training you to be *even better*."

Banner was greatly inspired by Carolyn Cullen. The concept of *even better* had already been her unwritten manifesto; the two women had a powerful soul connection that continues today. Their differences were equally great. Cullen had the blunt mannerisms of a roughneck; Banner had the total inability to look anything but feminine, whether she was wrestling fuel drums in a wrinkled men's shirt or loading a pickup with her long hair braided and sweat running down her cheeks. In city clothes she had the appearance and bearing of a Park Avenue secretary. Hidden behind her science-and-aviation education were strong artistic and literary skills. She wasn't ready to jump with both feet into a permanent career.

Cullen was more than twice Banner's age. Earlier in life she, too, had had many options, and she had chosen to cast herself in the role of an aviator, surrounded by women of like mind. The clay of which she was shaped had now dried and hardened. Banner on the other hand was in that youthful state of flux where neither life nor her own effort had yet congealed her.

The characteristics that Cullen saw as the makings of an even better pilot — Kitty's high energy, quick decisiveness, calmness under stress — were things that led her brother John to think that she could make hundreds of thousands of dollars a year in his business, the commodities market, as an arm-waving, bid-tossing broker in the great crowded hall

of the Chicago Board of Trade. When she compared that scene to the view beneath the airplane in Alaska, money lost its importance.

In contrast to Cullen's earthy speech, Banner speaks with well-bred Midwestern elocution, avoiding the use of expletives. Such clear articulation in a young woman can often come across as a social affectation, but it does not in Banner's case because of her way of punctuating her speech with brief, unselfconscious giggles. These instants are precious holdovers from growing up as a free spirit, and in them is the flip side of the imperious calm of the pilot. In these giggles is a woman who still dances until the sun comes up, writes letters to friends in calligraphy, runs for the swing in a children's playground, and skinny-dips on moonlit summer nights.

One of the world's greatest mountaineers says he will never fly with Banner again. He has no doubt about her competence. He believes that she is *even better*, but in a sense beyond that which Cullen intended. "To have that woman land you on a glacier, to get out of the plane, and to watch her fly off alone was entirely too much for me at the start of an expedition. Next time I'll fly with a man." Whether he does remains to be seen.

Cullen always had a strong feeling that Banner would end up flying in Alaska. She just knew it from the way Banner talked about dirt-strip landings in Washington State and about her short visit to Alaska when she was 19. The same wide-eyed spirit wasn't fully there when the subject switched to the East Coast, women's aviation, and cross-country powder puff derbies.

Banner came all too close to never flying in Alaska or anywhere else. She left Martha's Vineyard in 1975 and had a disheartening year. An accident on a lake near her family's summer home broke her back. She was para-sailing behind a power boat and hanging from a modified parachute, when a sudden cross wind shortly after takeoff caused the para-sail to descend rapidly; she caromed through an "unbreakable" fiberglass hull. During the same year David Rahm performed aerobatics on national television in the Middle East at the invitation of King Hussain and crashed fatally in front of the crowd. Banner decided to use her long convalescence to continue ground aviation training. Strapped in a back brace and also short of funds, she enrolled as the lone woman among three hundred men at Colorado Aerotech. All but a handful were on scholarships or Manpower grants, but she was turned down for every sort of aid, often because her education "overqualified" her. There were no Womanpower grants.

After four months of school her money ran out, and she left to go to work at the Boulder airport. There her luck turned; she was in the right place at the right time to meet Jim Sharp and accept his offer to work in Alaska.

The transition from working for a small air service to owning one was anything but easy. Banner arrived in Alaska late in 1976, and over the next two seasons she obtained commercial and float plane ratings while working for Sharp's air service. By 1978 she was in a quandry. Sharp's flying was in violation of some FAA flight regulations, but she felt a loyalty to him because of the opportunity she had been given. She decided to take a job away from Talkeetna until the situation was resolved. She worked for a large oil and mineral exploration firm's Anchorage office, expediting men and equipment to scores of camps throughout Alaska. Her good judgment paid off. The FAA sanctions she had feared forced Sharp to sell his air service. She didn't have the money to make an offer for it, so she continued to work for the mineral company.

Early in 1980 her opportunity came. Kimball Forrest, the student with whom she had once tried to hitch a plane to Ethiopia, was a geologist working for the mineral company. Both had been saving separately toward dreams of someday owning a bush flying business. They joined forces, arranged further financing, and bought out Holland Air Service, one of only three certified to fly out of Talkeetna.

After a busy 1980 season, they hope to expand their business beyond its present clientele of mountaineers and sightseers. Flight instruction and a second airplane are coming this year, and in the future they hope to offer float plane and larger Cessna 206 service, which could help them land contracts expediting people and equipment for both private companies and government agencies. Another possibility, making use of Forrest's background in geology, is to acquire the equipment for aerial photography and mapping.

There are tradeoffs in expanding what is now a seasonal business into a year-round operation. Banner now has the best of both worlds. From March to September she works the job of her dreams in Alaska. In the months in between, the telltale giggle broadens into another lifestyle that has included sailing a small boat through the Caribbean, skiing in Colorado, flying with her brothers for the fun of it, and plain hard work at the family boiler business in Chicago to keep up with the payments on her flying business. Her future now lies with the winds of the world, and the wings of her dreams. □

David Lokey photo

Galen Rowell photo

Bibliography

Books and Articles:

Davidson, Art. *Minus 148 Degrees: The First Winter Ascent of Mount McKinley*. The Mountaineers, Seattle, WA, 1999.

Dillard, Annie. *The Writing Life*. Harper Perennial, New York, NY, 1990.

Geeting, Doug and Steve Woerner. *Mountain Flying*. Tab Books Inc., Blue Ridge Summit, PA, 1988.

Greiner, James. *Wager with the Wind: The Don Sheldon Story*. St. Martin's Griffin Press, New York, NY, 1982.

Peterson, Wilferd, A. *The Art of Living*. Simon and Schuster, New York, NY, 1961.

Rowell, Galen. "Alaska's Lady Glacier Pilot." Alaskafest, June 1981.

Sfraga, Michael. *Bradford Washburn: A Life of Exploration*. Oregon State University Press, Corvallis, OR, 2004.

Sheldon, Roberta. *The Mystery of the Cache Creek Murders, A True Story*. Talkeetna Editions in association with Publication Associates, Anchorage, AK, 2001.

Sheldon, Roberta. *The Heritage of Talkeetna*. Talkeetna Editions, AK, 1995.

Turner, Janie. *Holding Her Head High*. Thomas Nelson, Inc., Nashville, TN, 2008.

Ziegler, Mel and Patricia. Foreword, *The Banana Republic Guide to Travel and Safari Clothing*, Ballantine Books, New York, NY, 1986.

Websites:

www.abbotsfordairshow.com
www.adfg.state.ak.us/pubs/notebook/
www.adn.com/section/alaska-life/we-alaskans/
www.aerofiles.com/_sk.html (Sorrell Aviation)
www.airliners.net/aircraft-data/stats.main?id=352
www.airweb.faa.gov (Regulatory and Guidance Library)
www.ankn.uaf.edu (Alaskan Native Knowledge Network)
www.answers.com (Seagull Energy Corporation)
www.articles.latimes.com/2003/jul/04/local/me-halaby4
www.ask.com
www.aviationweather.ws/051_Induction_System_Icing.php
www.cs.unm.edu/~forrest
www.climbing.about.com/od/mountainclimbing/a/K2FastFacts.htm
www.ethiopiamilitary.com/ethiopian-civil-war/
www.iditarod.com
www.iditarod.com/archives/musher/mushersummary_2638.html]
www.imdb.com/name/nm0000195/bio (Bill Murray)
www.independent.co.uk/news/obituaries/najeeb-halaby-548393.html
www.jukebox.uaf.edu/denali/html/tage.htm
www.kingcounty.gov/transportation/kcdot/Airport.aspx
www.klepperamerica.com/
www.knikarmbridge.com
www.law.umkc.edu/faculty/projects/ftrials/chicago7/chicago7.html
www.locogringo.com/chiapas/palenque.cfm
www.mayanmajix.com/13day_serpent_9.html
www.mexconnect.com/articles/1922-the-state-of-chihuahua-
    mexicoresource-page
www.moody.edu/
www.moviesunlimited.com/musite/product.asp?sku=D75819
www.patagonia.com
www.planeta.com/ecotravel/mexico/chihuahua/barrancas.html
www.planetware.com/mexico-city/plaza-garibaldi
www.roadtripamerica.com
www.saudiaramcoworld.com/issue/198906/jordan.s.royal.falcons.htm
www.setonshrine.org/bio/bio.htm (Eliz Seton, Saint)
www.sportsillustrated.cnn.com
www.sportsillustrated.cnn.com/vault/article/magazine/MAG1085841/2/index.
    htm.com
www.steliasguides.com/alaska
www.talkeetnatimes.com
www.talkeetnatimes.com (Talkeetna as Inspiration for Northern Exposure)
www.visitmexico.com/wb/Visitmexico/Visi_Palenque
www.washington.edu/alumni

Index

F

Fairhaven College, 21
Fisher, Laura, 12
Fisher, Mike, XXIII, XXV, 67, 76, 78, 96, 97, 102, 103, 111, 121, 128, 129, 131,
     132, 140, 151, 171, 172, 177, 199, 209, 219, 227, 257
Forrest, Kimball, XII, 97, 152, 155, 208, 260, 269
Forrest, Stephanie, 19, 32, 47
Fossett, Steve, 175, 177
Fulton, Bob, 193

G

Geeting Aviation, 101, 243, 251, 253
Geeting, Doug, XII, 96, 97, 101, 105, 169, 171, 176, 198, 205, 243, 248
Genet, Adrian, 148, 203, 247
Genet Expeditions, 104, 168, 173
Genet, Ray, 62, 63, 104, 123, 124, 133, 148, 168, 172, 231, 272
Genet, Taras, 145, 146, 148
Gillett, Ned, 237
Gochanour, Boyd, 185, 243
Griffin, Mary Beth, 45
Guimaraes, Suzanne, 78

H

Habeler, Peter, 173
Hackett, Peter, 228
Hamberger, Rudi, 134, 135
Hartzell, Nick, 96
Hillary, Sir Edmund, III, 238
Holland Air Service, 77, 167, 269
Holland, Ken, 77, 167, 188, 269
Homer, Ed, 97, 115, 205, 212
Hubert, Chris, 216
Hudson Air Service, 101
Hudson, Cliff, 97, 101, 118, 119, 143, 148, 150, 151, 184, 188, 207, 212, 235
Hudson, Jay, 247

J

Johnson, Brad, 117

K

K2 Aviation, 163, 173, 174, 175, 188, 195, 225, 256, 258, 260, 261, 264, 271
Kelly, Nancy, 15
King Hussein, 35, 37, 38

L

M

N

O

T

Talkeetna Air Taxi, XXIII, 51, 58, 73, 80, 132, 133, 134, 142, 156, 157, 269
Taylor, Ken, 208
Thomas, Lowell Jr., 97
Thompson, Frank, 12
Thorburn, Doug, 170
Thorburn, Scott, XII, 104, 170
Trade Winds, 49, 52
Trump, Nancy, 204
Twigg, Lynn, 96, 97

V

Vangalin, Tony, 266

W

Washburn, Barbara, 94
Washburn, Bradford, 94, 279
Wasson, John, 233
Wolff, John, 48, 52
Woods, Buddy, 158
Wright brothers, 93

Kitty in family Scout, 2017
Arcade photo

Photograph Credit:
All photographs are used with permission provided to the authors and are from the Seemann family and friends, unless otherwise noted.

Copyright © 2018 Kitty Banner Seemann

ISBN: 978-1-880654-51-4

Cover and Layout Design: Sonya Boushek
Publisher: Alan E. Krysan

An Imprint of Finney Company
www.finneyco.com

Printed in the United States of America

1 3 5 7 9 10 8 6 4 2